JAPANESE
BLITZ
On
DARWIN

February 19, 1942

John Thompson-Gray

Book cover design and layout
by Publicious Pty Ltd
www.publicious.com.au

Cataloguing-in-Publication data available from
the Australian Library of Congress

 ISBN: 978-0-9872585-0-2

Also available in ebook
ISBN: 978-0-9872585-1-9

Front cover pictures:
Planes - Wikipedia Public Domain
Bombed house - Bill Boyd Collection by courtesy of Bill Boyd Jnr.
Three ship photographs from From the Collection of Petty Officer H.E.S.
'Nobby' Clark by courtesy of Major Faye Clark WRAAC (ret.) OAM RFD.
SS *Neptuna* Explodes
HMAHS *Maununda* and lifeboat
USS *Peary*

Contents

CHAPTER 1

DARWIN TOWN AS A TARGET

INTRODUCTION

Darwin, located 12.27S, 130.50E was named in honour of Charles Darwin, British naturalist and author of *The Origin of Species.*

In 1942, the Australian Federal Government had jurisdiction over the Northern Territory with its centre of administration in Darwin.

The Imperial Japanese Navy Air Attack, which opened unannounced at Pearl Harbour on December 7th 1941, did a repeat performance at Darwin on February 19th 1942.

When Australians were defending their mainland for the first time, the only ally there when the whips were cracking was the United States of America. On that day, America and Australia were forged as *Cousins-in-Arms.*

SPIES

Japan had Spies afoot in Darwin. There were Spies throughout Australia since war was declared on Germany in September 1939. It was easy for Germans to look Dutch; Italians, American; Vichy French, Free French; and any of them, Australian.

According to Report MP729/6 from the Secret Correspondence files of the Departments of Defence and Army, "The NT and adjacent areas have been a hotbed of Japanese espionage….Darwin has become the centre of collation and communication of information…the possibility of these agents being clothed in Australian, USA or NEI uniforms should not be ignored." The report focuses on a fifth column, with missionaries of German and Spanish origin coercing their indigenous parishioners with promises of liberation.

There were over 1,000 Japanese in Broome and Darwin because the stamina of Japanese divers was essential for the Australian Pearling Industry. By February 1942, 200 Japanese were interned on the Tiwi Islands and many were sent home.

A characteristic of Japanese army boots was dual caps, one for the big toe and one for the rest. The distinctive footprint left by this boot was frequently observed around Darwin but never the wearer. Parachutes were spotted but never a parachutist. Targets were being marked, often at night using headlights. Examples occurred at Livingstone Airfield and a Signals Company opposite an Ordnance yard in Darwin.

RAAF Base in Darwin had an experimental radar station, almost operational by February 1942. It was installed at Dripstone Caves with a dedicated telephone line to Headquarters. The cable was sabotaged an hour before the first raid.

The Allies had their own agents and military intelligence. Locally, that included reports from aircraft, submarines, ships and coast-watchers.

At 9am on February 17th, 48 hours before the first raid on Darwin, David Ross, the Australian Consul to Portuguese East Timor in Dili, reported "Suspected aircraft carrier activity in the Banda Sea north of Wetar Island." It was known to Allied Intelligence that Nagumo Force carriers were stationed at Cavite on the 15th February when Singapore fell. If these were the carriers reported by Ross, the presence of such a huge formation travelling from Cavite through the Banda Sea would be saying 'Darwin AND Timor AND Bali.' RAAF set out to test the reliability of this information. The first direct sighting of the four carriers was radioed in by an American Catalina at 10:15am on Thursday, February 19th, seventeen minutes into the Battle of Darwin.

GOVERNMENT

The Curtin government was elected on October 3rd 1941. They were only four months into their first term when Japan attacked Australia at Darwin.

The Commonwealth Government administered the Northern Territory through Aubrey Abbott who had been Administrator of the Territory for five years leading up to the battle. He lived with his family at Government House, located beach-side on the Esplanade at Fort Hill, a conspicuous target. His administration building shared the Esplanade precinct with others: Post Master General, Post Office, Overland Telegraph Station, submarine cable from Java, Police Station and Barracks, Court House, Town Hall and others in the same cluster. Behind the Esplanade were secondary targets in the commercial centre including depots, service outlets, market, shops, offices, hotel, China-town, churches, railway station, schools and utilities.

Judge Alexander Wells administered justice from the courthouse. He gave advice to the Administrator and took an interest in the management of Fannie Bay Gaol. The policy he applied to prisoners will be revealed when the bombs start dropping.

The Northern Australia Workers Union (N.A.W.U.) was militant, detested Aubrey Abbott and faced-off with UK food company Vestey Brothers. Union membership was always 100% and Wharfie ranks recently swelled to 270 hoping that this would stevedore military cargo quicker. The problem wasn't manpower. Rolling stock access to and from the wharf had to negotiate a right angle bend on a turntable, teams of Wharfies in the tropical heat manually dragging the loaded trucks on and off it two at a time. The Wharf had no crane; cargo was handled on ships' derricks requiring lighter sling loads and therefore more lifts. The cause of the problem was mostly the system, a little bit the Wharfies.

In 1871 the overseas telegraph link was completed with the installation of a submarine cable from Java to Darwin. It was coupled to the Overland Telegraph Line in 1872, connecting Canberra and London.

MUNICIPAL UTILITIES
Water, Power and Sewerage

Manton Dam 35mi south of Darwin was constructed in 1939 and was always a likely target. Water from the dam was stored in steel tanks, five were elevated tanks located in Darwin, one an elevated tank at RAAF Base and one a ground level tank at Stokes Hill. In 1940 additional tanks met the growing military demand and reticulation was underway.

In 1941, Commander A.E. (Chook) Fowler RAN, with the help of his Army engineers, installed plant and pipes to pump water from Manton Dam to Darwin. The Royal Australian Navy held exclusive rights to one of the pipes Chook laid. Another of his missions was defence of the town water supply and the pumping plant had been located accordingly. As a practice run for yet another of his missions, Chook installed a double anti-torpedo boom-net 30ft from the concrete retaining wall of the dam.

In 1939 a large power station was constructed at the top of Frances Bay, off Armidale Street in Stuart Park. Its defence relied on guards to foil sabotage and heavy sandbagging to defend it from air raids and naval guns. By 1940 increased military demand was overloading the power station so a second plant was constructed nearby in Bishop Street.

In 1939 septic sewerage became mandatory for all new housing in Myilly. Apart from this, municipal night-soil collection serviced the town and suburbs. *The Dunny Truck* crew consisted of the driver, Ludo Dalby and two doffers to operate both sides of the street at the same time. At least there was no sewerage treatment plant for an enemy to bomb.

HOSPITALS

At the time of the first air raid, Darwin had seven hospitals. There were three civilian hospitals: a recently abandoned old hospital, a new hospital at Myilly and a Leprosarium on Channel Island. There were four military hospitals: the RAAF Base hospital, an Army field hospital at Berrimah, an Army general hospital at Bagot and the Army hospital ship HMAHS *Manunda* at anchor in the harbour.

The old Darwin Hospital was built in Packard Street overlooking Doctors Gully. The first construction in 1874 was upgraded with stone in 1878. By the 1930's it was not capable of supplying the demand for hospital beds and the range of medical treatment required by a civilian population approaching 4,000.

The Administrator of Health Darwin, Dr C E Cook had a professionally prepared plan including blueprints for a new 89-bed hospital on a site at Lambell Terrace, Myilly. Cook's enthusiasm, however, was no match for the Depression.

In April 1939 the Commonwealth Department of Health in Canberra assumed responsibility for all health services in the Northern Territory. Cook was transferred but his plan was still on the table. Soon after, a medical centre and hospital for aborigines commenced at Bagot. Nearby, RAAF Base had its own hospital.

After the senior officers of the three armed forces in Darwin laid their careers on the line with Canberra,

Cook's plan was adopted and construction at Myilly commenced in January 1941. The Army installed a General Hospital at Berrimah looking down Runway 29 at the air field, one mile from its threshold. In the emergency following Pearl Harbour, the Army moved the Aboriginal Centre at Bagot to Delissaville and the Bagot site became a small general hospital.

The new Darwin hospital opened at Myilly on February 2nd 1942, a few hundred yards from the Larrakeyah Army Barracks and seventeen days from being bombed.

Manunda arrived to fuel in Darwin on January 12th en route to Singapore. She was held up by marshalling operations for the Houston Convoy and eventually by the deteriorating military situation in South East Asia. *Manunda* was originally built for Adelaide Steam Ship Company by Wm. Beardmores of Glasgow and later converted into a hospital ship. She had three hospital wards and boasted five operating theatres.

AWA COASTAL RADIO NETWORK

Amalgamated Wireless (Australasia) Limited (AWA) had a radio network in Australia. Eighteen coastal radio stations were broadcasting to wireless sets and providing two-way radio communications to remote cattle stations, the Royal Flying Doctor Service, shipping, missions, Royal Australian Airforce (RAAF), Royal Australian Navy (RAN) and the national network of the Department of Civil Aviation. The 18 coastal stations also acted as feeders for the landline telegraph system.

Lou Curnock at Aeradio Station VID transmitted from Frog's Hollow in Darwin providing communications to many outposts including Father John McGrath at Nguiu Catholic Mission in the southeast corner of Bathurst Island and Brother Edward Bennett of Pirlangimpi Catholic Mission on Melville Island. Curnock also had a frequency on which he could speak directly with RAAF operations at the airfield.

DEPARTMENT OF CIVIL AVIATION

Bruce Ackland and Ted Betts were officers of the Department of Civil Aviation (DCA) at the Civilian aerodrome next to RAAF Base. Their responsibilities included radio communications and civilian flight operations.

Darwin had a flying boat harbour in Frances Bay with slipway and passenger terminal just north of Stokes Hill. The Officer in Charge of the base was William Wake. DCA ferried passengers to and from the flying boats in shuttle tenders crewed by Lieutenant Ian McRoberts and Coxswain John Waldie. All these DCA officers were recognised for their bravery during the Battle of Darwin particularly Waldie who, showing no concern for his own safety, won the British Empire Medal (Civil Division) for rescuing 150 sailors from certain death.

AIR RAID PRECAUTIONS

After 1939 the civil administration formed a Darwin Air Raid Precautions Unit (ARP) with Edgar Harrison as Officer-in-Charge. Harrison appointed wardens and began the work of educating citizens and coordinating emergency services. The Unit installed air raid sirens around town, helped citizens to prepare slit trenches and organised practice drills. The programme developed as citizens asked for more and better information. For example, in the advent of Darwin being occupied, the first leg *evacuating south* to Adelaide was 1,000 miles south to Alice Springs on *Leaping Lena*, the train to Larrimah; then from Larrimah to the Alice on the dirt road servicing the Overland Telegraph Line. The Afghan Express railway ran 1,200mi *south* from Alice Springs to Adelaide with the Overland Telegraph Line and service road beside it. This became the general meaning when anyone said *"evacuate south."*

ARP developed a plan which prioritised evacuees by partitions of women, children, the old, sick and others. Part of their plan was 'reserved occupations' which defined the people who had to stay until the last minute. This eventually proved useful when 63 women in nursing and telegraphy held their posts throughout the Blitz.

A state of emergency was declared in Darwin after Japan attacked Pearl Harbour and the administrator told Harrison to evacuate Darwin. All hell broke loose. Many citizens tried to queue-jump and would not take instructions from ARP wardens. Abbott confounded the whole process by ordering that evacuation be based on addresses and that all evacuation was to be by sea. This turned the carefully prepared ARP plan on its head. When Judge Wells ruled that ARP wardens had no legal authority to order citizens to evacuate, it was the last straw for Harrison and the ARP folded. The heads of the three armed forces convened as the Darwin Defence Coordination Committee (DDCC), brushed Abbott and his administrators aside, and took over where the ARP left off.

The DDCC had the Red Cross giving lectures on anti-gas equipment, first aid and air raid precautions. When the Army hospital ship *Manunda* arrived on January 12th 1942 and seemed to be held up, it provided a special opportunity for the DDCC. Medical personnel were training in triage and intensive care while exchanging visits with all the other hospitals including hospitals in ships. By Wednesday February 18th they were well drilled in rescue and evacuation operations by air, land and sea to *Manunda*.

Town air raid sirens were wired to RAAF Base so that warnings would sound at the earliest possible time.

EVACUATION

Eventually 3,000 citizens out of 5,000 were evacuated from Darwin Town leaving 2,000 to provide essential services. Meanwhile the number of Service personnel in the area jumped to 15,000.

DDCC was evacuating civilians through Darwin, to southern ports by ship and to Adelaide or inland locations by rail and road. Ships accounted for the evacuation of 1066 women and 900 children. Army ships arriving with troops and military cargo were back-loaded with evacuees. *Zealandia* took 530, *Koolinda* 302, *Montoro* 187 and *Koolama* 173.

Within eight hours of the attack on Pearl harbour the Imperial Japanese Navy was blockading the Philippines. *President Grant*, a luxury passenger liner in Manila Harbour received an order to 'sail to the nearest friendly port'. She arrived in Darwin December 23rd and quickly sold 166 first class tickets at £18 for passage to southern ports.

Leaping Lena departed for Larrimah railway station daily. Evacuation overland was favoured by non-Europeans, and many went short distances only, to bush towns and camps.

CHAPTER 2
HARBOUR DEFENCE

The defence of ships in the harbour depended on harbour characteristics, ship numbers, distribution, manoeuvrability, experience, weapon systems, friendly fire power, enemy strength and weapons.

The characteristics of Harbour defence were being improved by the Navy.

Soon after the declaration of War in 1939 the German Navy became active in Australian Waters and the Royal Australian Navy started to install Harbour Defences at key ports around the coast. A map of Darwin Harbour shows its key features: Frances Bay, East Arm, Middle Arm, West Arm and its entrance. It was 12mi at its widest, 18mi at its longest and 3.5mi from East Point to West Point at its entrance.

The shoreline was a mixture of mangroves, beaches, cliffs and the wharf area in the inner port ran from Stokes Hill around to Fort Hill. The coast and waters of the harbour were infested with crocodiles, sharks and box jelly fish. The main channel from the entrance to the wharf was comparatively wide and Lieutenant John Bell, Harbour Master, had mooring buoys laid out on the north and south sides

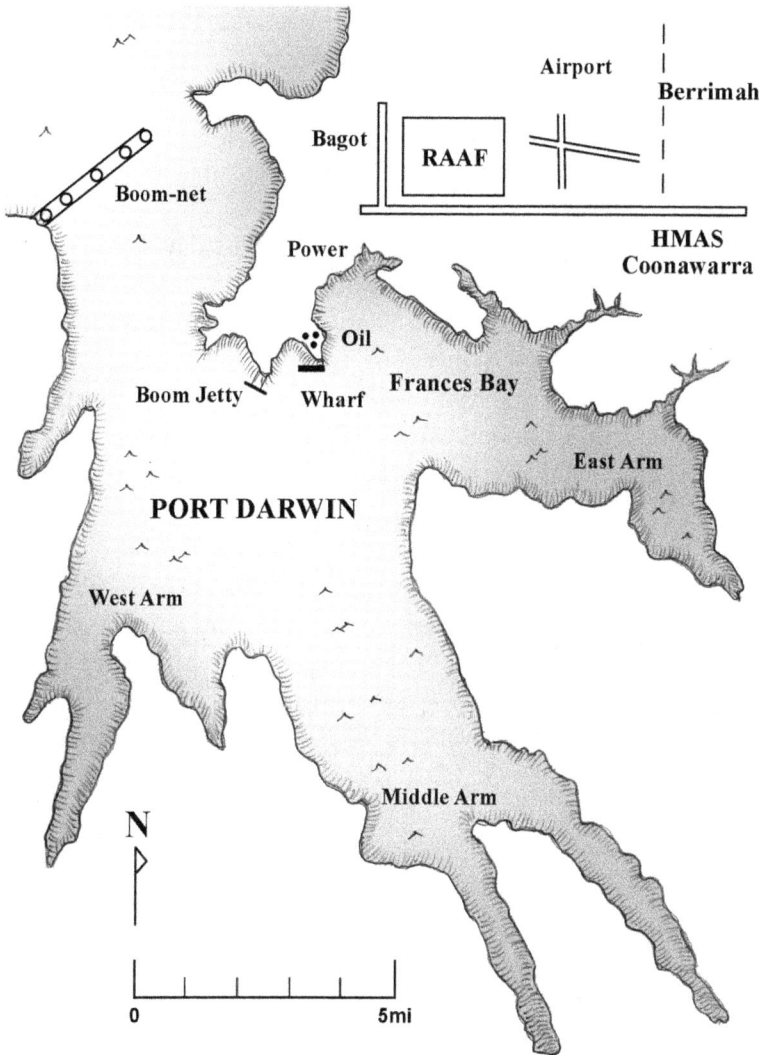

Map of Port Darwin

of the channel forming two concentric arcs, the outer arc continuing into the channel up East Arm.

Tides were typically 20ft and ebbed up to 4kn. On the day of Battle it was high tide at 8am and the attack started at 10am.

Although it was still the Wet season, Thursday February 20th started as a clear fine day; a typical long white cloud at 2,500ft developed 5mi inland by 9:30am; and cloud cover at the Harbour increased to 3/8 by 10:30am. By then the harbour was full of dense smoke from a burning oil tank farm, exploded cargos, sinking ships and burning debris, all moving down harbour with the fire-tide.

At Darwin, Commander A.E. (Chook) Fowler had independent command of 20 officers, 400 ratings and 6 vessels. His HQ at the base of Fort Hill had small jetties to berth his vessels and shore depots for his materials and tooling. His main mission, a double meshed-steel-wire anti-submarine, anti-torpedo Boom-net was under construction between East Point and West Point of the entrance, a distance of 5.59km. Stage one, recently completed, was 4.46km long, the top of the cable being held up by buoys, anchored at regular intervals to the sea bed. There were six Boom-net construction vessels as well as seven Boom-net defence vessels, mainly corvettes of the 20th Mine Sweeping Flotilla. The opening in the boom was used by friendly vessels. HMAS *Kara Kara,* a former Sydney vehicle ferry, and HMAS *Kookaburra* were permanently anchored gate ships. These vessels were backed up by RAN minesweepers and boom vessels *Tolga, Terka, Koala, Kangaroo* and *Karangi.*

Heavy artillery emplacements were strategically located on shore to deal with approaching enemy vessels and provide defensive fire for the Boom-net. The 2/14th had four High Angle AA emplacements, two on the coast, and Lewis guns on the oil tanks. Machine gunners of the 19th were defending the beaches and fuel tanks which were camouflaged into cliffs.

Germany attacked Australian assets with mines, ships and submarines. The Boom-net was part of this kind of warfare, but somewhat redundant for Japan's new kind of warfare deploying aircraft in strength to strike enemy ships.

The wharf and oil tank farm were included in saturation bombing but Val dive bombers and Zero fighters delivered three bombing raids across the Harbour. Most ships in the harbour had machine guns or light AA guns suitable against these attacks. For example, HMAS *Warrego* was an escort sloop of the Grimsby Class, with twin and single four inch gun mountings and a four barrel 0.5" Vickers machine gun.

There were 45 ships in harbour the day of the attack, one British and one Norwegian Oiler on charter to the US Asia Fleet, 6 American ships and the rest Australian. The rate of arrival of ships had been greater than the rate at which the primitive wharf facilities could turn them around. For this reason the mooring buoys close to the inner harbour were overcrowded.

The US Asia Fleet was retreating from the Philippines to Darwin for fuelling, provisioning and maintenance on their way to Java. For example, in one week 8 submarines, 3 cruisers and 8 destroyers arrived. Japanese reconnaissance flights and Spies in Darwin must have been having a field day. As a second example, on February 10th 1942, Japanese reconnaissance photographs showed 30 aircraft, an aircraft carrier (USS *Langley*), 5 destroyers, 21 merchant Vessels, a PBY tender with her clutch of Catalinas and all the usual Australian ships. PBY is a Patrol Boat fighting Catalina manufactured by Consolidated Industries Ltd (USA).

Some crews were battle hardened, experienced in the defence of merchant ships as well as their own. For example, on December 8th 1941 Japanese aircraft attacked destroyer USS *Peary* at her berth in the Cavite Navy Yard in the Philippines. Her superstructure was riddled killing 8 and starting fires. Torpedo warheads were stacked on the wharf beside her, the wharf was ablaze but she was towed to safety before the wharf blew up. Peary was next attacked by the Japanese on December 26th while at sea on her way to join USS *Houston,* and next by friendly fire on 28th December in Makassar Strait when her radio failed, and next on 29th December by Japanese bombs and torpedoes. The officers decided to paint her metallic appearance green with palm tree artwork on the hull. *Peary* became the tattooed destroyer. She set course to meet Houston in Darwin.

The harbour was clogged but the ships were also close packed. For example, USS *William B. Preston* had to escape from East Arm on a path through the other ships. She could not manoeuvre freely to frustrate attacking bombers.

It was difficult to defend unloaded convoy ships carrying troops and military cargo. MV *Admiral Halstead* and USAT *Meigs* departed Hawaii for the Philippines on December 3rd 1941. They carried a Battalion of the 148th Idaho Field Artillery Regiment, a hundred Army Air Corp specialists, army trucks, Kittyhawks, aviation gasoline, railway lines, weapons and ammunition to reinforce General Douglas MacArthur. They were too late and ordered to return to the USA. The US President, Franklin D. Roosevelt over-ruled these orders diverting the ships to Java via Australia.

The Boom was redundant, the characteristics of the harbour were exploited by the enemy, the port was clogged, ships were close packed preventing manoeuvrability, unloaded merchantmen were vulnerable, the enemy attacked in force with accurate bombing and gun fire but ships were armed with some support from land based AA and machine gun emplacements.

CHAPTER 3
RAAF AND ARMY TARGETS

RAAF Base was 4mi northeast of the town centre and 4mi east from the Boom-net. It housed RAAF operations but Combined Area Headquarters of the Allied Strike Force for the defence of the Dutch East Indies moved into the same site. The Allies had put all their eggs in one basket.

RAAF Base was not a permanently armed asset, rather, a staging centre with maintenance workshops. Hudson Bomber Squadron 2 based at Penfoi and Squadron 13 based at Ambon cycled their aircraft into Darwin for routine maintenance. Squadron 12 Wirraway Fighters supporting the Hudsons also dropped in for maintenance but parked at the civil aerodrome to use its longer runway. Prior to battle day, 9 freshly maintained Wirraways had relocated 48mi south at Batchelor aerodrome. Three Wirraways were still being serviced in Darwin increasing risk of attack for the civil aerodrome.

The American-British-Dutch-Australian strike force for the defence of the Dutch East Indies (ABDA) promoted Wing Commander Frederick Scherger from Station Commander to Group Captain at Combined Area Headquarters in Darwin. Scherger's replacement as Station Commander was a Reserve Wing Commander, Sturt Griffith. ABDA, formed on January 18th, had set up its headquarters in Java that day with General Sir Archibald Wavell, Air Vice-Marshal Sir Richard Williams and Admiral Karel Doorman. Williams wanted to return to Britain and Scherger was ambitious.

On February 18th, the day before the attack, Captain Penry Thomas, Naval Officer in Charge at Darwin told Scherger in confidence that Williams was in Darwin town to brief him, Scherger, the following morning.

Scherger undermined Griffith's authority in front of the enlisted men. On the day, it was Griffith's hand on the air raid sirens, too reluctant to hit the button for fear of being ridiculed if it were a false alarm. The Lowe Royal Commission found Scherger responsible for RAAF failure to raise the alarm before the Town was attacked. This may seem a poetic finding, but a case for Scherger will be argued later when we learn more about Commander Mitsui Fuschida.

On December 22nd 1941 the Chief of Staff of the US Army Air Corp, General George C Marshall declared Darwin a US Army and Navy Base. With the fall of the Philippines, reinforcing Singapore and the Dutch East Indies became the new Allied priority; but as US assets were being rushed to Java via Darwin, losses were significant. Only 37 of 85 Kittyhawks made it to Java, the main cause being pilot inexperience.

Pursuit Squadron 3 was a sad loss. On Tuesday February 10th when the United States Air Force 3rd Pursuit Squadron left Darwin for Timor, it had to leave behind pilots Lieutenant Robert Buel and Lieutenant Robert Oestreicher with their non-operational P-40E Kittyhawks. The squadron departed RAAF Base for Koepang on Tuesday February 10th navigated by an LB-30 Liberator. Owing to bad weather, it took so long for the Liberator to find Penfoi airport that the 8 Kittyhawks ran out of fuel and crashed killing the pilots.

Pursuit Squadron 17 (Provisional) is another case in point. The President of the United States sent *Admiral Halstead* to Australia and she ended up in Brisbane on December 22nd where 25 crated P-40E Kittyhawks could be assembled by her airforce technicians, flown to Perth and shipped as deck cargo to Java. Sabotage was suspected with parts missing for gun sights and no engine coolant. Eventually, 15 Kittyhawks were assembled at Amberley as Pursuit Squadron 17 (Provisional) under the command of Major Floyd (Slugger) Pell. Five had engine failure and crashed, ten were flown by inexperienced pilots as far as Port Pirie in South Australia where one crashed trying to land and the rest were diverted to support the *Houston* convoy out of Darwin. The squadron arrived in Darwin on the afternoon of February 15th, the convoy having sailed that morning under orders from Admiral Doorman.

There were about 12,000 Army personnel in Darwin. The 23rd Australian Infantry Brigade was in town and many were accommodated at Larrakeyah Barracks next to the new Darwin hospital at Myilly on Cullen Bay. There were at least a thousand army personnel still on troop ships in the harbour waiting to unload, and the Army hospital ship *Manunda* was in port.

The 2/14th heavy AA Battalion had sixteen High Angle guns in four emplacements, each emplacement with four guns sharing a 360 degree arc of fire. Their salvos at 20 rounds per minute had a horizontal range of 11mi and were capable at 30,000ft where Japanese bombers fly. The emplacements were the Oval in Town, Francis Bay, McMillan and Berrimah. The guns were defended by revetment walls and

Lewis machine guns which were potent against dive bomber and fighter attack. Eight of their Lewis Guns were located to defend the oil tanks at the harbour.

Elliot Point and the Quarantine Station were defended by light 3in AA guns. Customs' Examination Steamer *Southern Cross* was based at the Quarantine Station.

The 19th Machine Gun Regiment was deployed to defend the beach and tanks. The soldiers of this unit like Rex Ruwoldt were brave Victorian teenagers camped near a beach infested by mosquitoes, flies, centipedes and scorpions, where the crocodile that takes you is the one you never see.

The 4th commando company was part of the infantry build up. Overall, there was only one rifle for every five soldiers and each soldier had been issued with one clip of five bullets.

CHAPTER 4

FRONT LINE

In South East Asia Japan was driving the front line south with rapid success. At the outbreak of hostilities at Pearl Harbour, all US navy and military were signalled, 'Japan has commenced hostilities. Govern yourself accordingly.' Ships in the Philippines received this message at 5:30am local time and were under attack by dawn. Japan now controlled timber-getting from the Philippine forests and Allied sanctions were gone.

On December 10th 1941, in the Gulf of Siam, Japanese Nell bombers sank the capital battle ship HMS *Prince of Wales* and cruiser HMS *Repulse* which arrived too late to block Japanese landings in North Malaya. Japan now had rubber trees and the Allied sanctions were gone.

On January 11th Japan captured Miri in Sarawak enabling quick control over major oil fields at Brunei and Tarakan. Japan now had enough oil and the Allied sanctions were irrelevant.

Vice Admiral Osami Nagumo led the school of thought that Japan should focus on taking Australia with its vast agricultural and strategic assets. On the other hand, Admiral Isoroku Yamamoto, who was the Commander-in-Chief of the Pearl Harbour invasion force, led the school of thought that Japan should lure the American

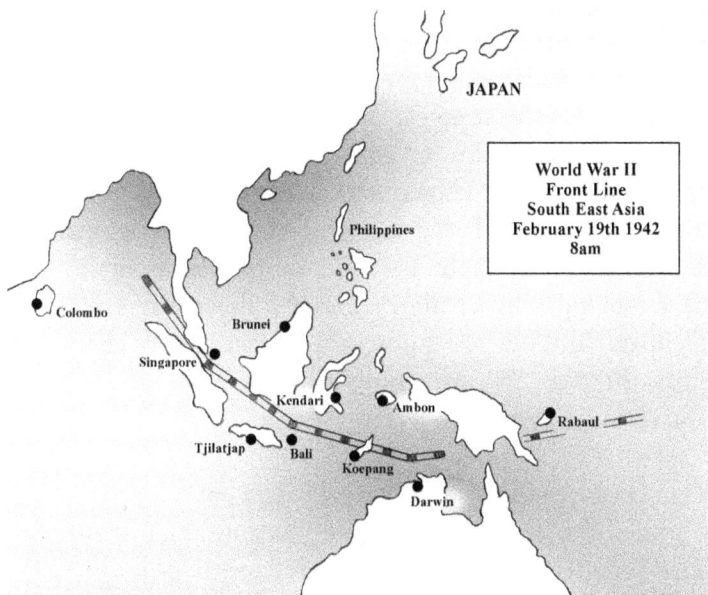

World War ll Front Line

carriers, all of which survived Pearl Harbour, to an air and sea battle at Midway in the North Pacific. On that footing Nagumo was pleased to receive orders to reposition northeast of New Guinea and there, between January 20th and 23rd, take the Australian Territory of Rabaul in New Britain and Kavieng in New Ireland. This left the Moluccas and Timor untenable.

In the Dutch East Indies the islands of Sumatra and Java run in an arc from Burma to Bali forming a 2,200 mile land barrier between the South China Sea and Indian Ocean. Were it not for Sunda Strait between the eastern end of Sumatra and the western end of Java the inconvenience to shipping would be similar to that before the Suez or Panama canals. Key Allied naval bases in Java were at Tanjung Priok (Batavia) and Surabaya both on the north side of the island facing Singapore. The Allies were well aware of the strategic importance of having a base on the south side of Java to control shipping through Sunda Strait. Their only choice was Tjilatjap where the build up of Allied naval and air power was coming through Australian ports. Fighters could fly from Darwin to Java by refuelling at Koepang in Timor followed by a refuel at Denpasar in Bali. As hubs in this vital supply chain, the front line was moving rapidly towards Bali, Koepang and Darwin.

On February 4th after several days of combat Japan captured the island of Ceram and its naval base at Ambon. The Imperial Japanese Navy moved up Mitsubishi G3M ('Nell') bombers and C5M reconnaissance aircraft. In the days that followed Japan walked into the Celebes almost unopposed and set up a base at Kendari. They quickly moved in Mitsubishi G4M ('Betty') bombers. The north of Australia was now within range of land based Japanese aircraft. These advances forced Allied withdrawals to Singapore, Java, Timor and Darwin, the new front line. Within a fortnight, Nells from Ceram and Bettys from Kendari would be bombing RAAF Base Darwin.

On Sunday February 15th Vice Admiral Osami Nagumo's force was made up of Imperial Japanese Navy Carrier Division 1 with his flag carrier *Akagi* and carrier *Kaga* as well as Division 2 with carriers *Hiryu* and *Soryu*. His carriers were four of the six deployed against Pearl Harbour and his naval commander was Mitsuo Fuchida who led the air attack at Pearl Harbour. Nagumo Force was anchored at Palauig, a port on the western side of Luzon, North Philippines. It was supporting the naval blockade of the Philippines and acting in reserve for Japan's attack on Singapore.

When Singapore fell that day it was Nagumo's cue for the next step towards Colombo which was the fallback port for the British after Singapore. To defeat the British in Colombo would destroy their last hold over the Indian Ocean. That next step was Darwin and Nagumo Force weighed anchor for the Arafura Sea, supported by two battle ships, two cruisers and one light cruiser.

CHAPTER 5
HOUSTON CONVOY

On February 12th, General George Betts gathered the *Houston* convoy in Darwin to carry reinforcements to Timor. The 3rd pursuit squadron had departed Darwin for Timor two days earlier and Betts had been planning to use them as air cover for the *Houston* convoy. They could still provide cover flying out of Penfoi airfield. As we have already discovered the third pursuit squadron had two Kittyhawks under repair at Darwin and the other eight had crashed in bad weather trying to land at Penfoi. The convoy was now waiting for Pursuit Squadron 17 (Provisional) to arrive from Port Pirie to provide air cover for the convoy. The convoy had to wait because there were no other aircraft around, and Pursuit Squadron 17 could be diverted from their flight to Perth.

With the fall of Singapore on Sunday February 15th Admiral Karel Doorman, Commander-in-Chief of American-British-Dutch-Australian Strike Force (ABDA) for the defence of the Dutch East Indies, issued orders for *Houston* under Captain Albert H. Rooks to sail.

Houston was a heavy cruiser, once the flagship of the US Navy and recently the flagship of Admiral Thomas Hart of the US Asia Fleet. In the Battle of Makassar Straits on February 4th she lost an 8" gun turret, the explosion killing 48 sailors, injuring 20. The cause was clear. Defective ammunition at her 5in guns had stopped

Heavy Cruiser USS Houston

covering fire for the turret. On this convoy to Timor she had fresh ammunition and was screened by her dedicated destroyer *Peary* with two well armed anti-submarine minesweepers *Warrego* and HMAS *Swan*.

The other four in the convoy were Army transports. USAT *Meigs* and SS *Mauna Loa* were carrying an Australian anti-tank unit and the 2/4th Pioneer Battalion of the Australian Infantry Force. Meigs had been hanging around in Darwin since February 5th waiting for convoy. Mauna Loa was part of a plan to run supplies to Makassar en route to the Philippines. She became available for this convoy when the scheme was dropped.

USAT *Port Mar* and MV *Tulagi* were carrying specialist units and the first battalion of the US 148th Field Artillery Regiment of the Idaho National Guard. *Port Mar* arrived to unload stores for US forces already in Darwin. *Tulagi,* an Australian vessel under Captain J. Thomson, after evacuating civilians from New Guinea, had been sent with supplies to Darwin. Because of the bottle neck at the Wharf both vessels were waiting in the queue, still loaded and ready to convoy.

These troops with all their military equipment were heading for the garrison at Koepang. It was not long before the convoy was being followed by a Kawanishi H6K flying boat ('Mavis') from the 21st Flotilla based at the Imperial Japanese Navy's newly captured base in Ceram. *Houston* delivered high altitude anti aircraft fire. In return the Mavis dropped two 60kg bombs but missed. *Houston* broke radio silence calling for air support from Darwin to shoot it down.

By the afternoon of February 15th the two Kittyhawks left behind at Darwin by the 3rd Pursuit Squadron were operational and pilots Buel and Oestreicher were patrolling the Darwin defence zone. Buel intercepted the call from *Houston* and responded. Oestreicher, whose radio was out of order, wasn't sure what was going on and continued the patrol over Darwin.

Buel quickly found the convoy 100nmi from Darwin and the Mavis made a run for it. Lookouts on the convoy lost sight of the two aircraft and Buel's radio went dead. His last message said he had hit the Mavis. Lookouts saw a puff of grey smoke on the horizon but Buel's fate remained a mystery. Five of the nine Mavis crew survived, drifted in a life-raft for 5 days and came ashore on Melville Island. They were soon captured by Tiwi Islanders who handed them over to Army authorities. The Japanese pilots refused to be interrogated, seeing the war out at Cowra Prisoner of War Camp in New South Wales. In 1985 one of the repatriated prisoners, Marekuni Takahara, told the true story of Buel's fate. The Mavis rear gunner and Buel had simultaneously shot one another down, the Kittyhawk descending as a smoking fireball into the sea. There was no parachute; Buel was still in his cockpit where he burnt to death.

As Oestreicher returned from local patrol and landed at RAAF Base, Major Floyd Pell arrived with nine Kitty Hawks diverted at Port Pirie in South Australia to support the *Houston* convoy.

After losing track of *Houston* overnight the Japanese Navy pinpointed her location in the Timor Sea 280 nautical miles west of Darwin. Their attack resumed in full force with 45 planes. Again, Houston radioed for air support from Darwin. She spun quickly leaving a stick of bombs in her wake. Her fire-power, blazing to every altitude and attack pattern thrown at her, released incessant streaks of angry fire that lit her up like a Christmas tree. She forced Japanese planes to stay up high.

Major Pell led six Kittyhawks to provide air cover for Houston but by the time they found the convoy the battle was over. *Houston* supported by *Peary, Warrego, Swan* and heavy machine gun fire from the 148th on *Tulagi* put down an anti aircraft barrage that forced the attackers away but some persisted. *Houston* circled further from the convoy to lure Japanese planes away from the troop ships. Every Japanese pilot was desperate for the battle honour of sinking their 'enemy number one'. *Houston* took a hit but her deadly fire power and skilful avoiding action kept her from further harm. Eventually the attacking aircraft departed. The convoy suffered minor damage only with no transports sunk. *Mauna Loa* was damaged when near misses riddled the port lifeboats, holed her hull and sent fragment strikes as high as the wheel house injuring two seamen.

At 3:15pm, before the convoy could regroup, General Sir Archibald Wavell from ABDA headquarters in Java ordered its return to Darwin because the current battle had drained the Convoy's ammunition stocks and further air attacks without adequate air cover were likely.

The convoy returned on February 18th and signalled to everyone that Darwin's turn was coming.

USS Houston and USS Peary returning to Port Darwin after ABDA withdrew their convoy February 18th 1942 - From the Collection of Petty Officer H.E.S. 'Nobby' Clark by courtesy of Major Faye Clark WRAAC (ret.) OAM RFD.

CHAPTER 6
FUSCHIDA'S PLAN

Fuschida's planning group must have been pleased with the layout of strategic targets in Darwin. The main strip at RAAF Base was aligned with the infrastructure hub next door at Berrimah; the Harbour southwest of RAAF Base was packed with 46 vessels including the greatest prize of all, *Houston*; in between, the targets of Town and Inner Port were in line, one line.

Strategically, the Civil Airfield as well as RAAF Base had to be demolished mainly because of its infrastructure but also because it housed RAAF Wirraway fighters which needed the longer runway at Civil Airfield. RAAF Base had become the maintenance centre for land-based Allied aircraft operating out of Northern Australia, Timor and, until recently, Ceram and the Celebes. Its workshops and spare parts inventory were significant. The Base was also a fuelling point for United States Army Air Corp (USAAC) planes on their way to Java via Timor and Bali. Intelligence from Air Reconnaissance and Japanese Agents in Darwin confirmed 10 Kittyhawk fighters at the Base with a few bombers including a B-17E Flying Fortress. Destruction of the Base required High-Altitude saturation bombing by Kate, Nell and Betty bombers and 27 of each were allocated.

Precision bombing was needed for specific targets at Berrimah and Civil Airfield: 18 Val dive-bombers (17 on the day) with 9 screening Zeros were required.

Kittyhawk fighters were capable at the altitude ceiling of Japanese bombers and this risk had to be eliminated before bombing began. A squadron of nine Zeros was assigned to remove Kittyhawks from the battle. Because RAAF Base was only 4 miles inland from the Boom-net at East Point, this squadron could create a diversion by approaching from the northwest to shoot-up the Boom Defence Vessels on its way to RAAF Base.

Strategic targets along the Shore ran from Stokes Hill Wharf and Oil Tank Farm at one end to the Larrakeyah Military Barracks at the other end. The bombing zone on Town and Shore was 600 yards wide and 3 miles long. This was ideal for high density bombing and 54 Kates were allocated. Some precision bombing and strafing by Val dive bombers would be useful against anti-aircraft emplacements, searchlights and targets of opportunity.

Some ships were clustered around the inner port. Two parallel sets of buoys were strung along the outer port at 2,000 and 3,000 yards from the wharf. Ships were individual targets requiring precision bombing; 54 Val dive bombers and 18 Zeros were required. Why 72 aircraft and 162 bombs against 46 ships? It should be enough to make sure Houston was sunk given that she held off 45 planes a couple of days earlier.

The bottom line was 232 aircraft, 645 bombs, no torpedoes, attacking in coordinated waves.

It was logical for Japan to come from the northwest. True

to Japanese spirit Fuschida took the logical and reversed it, attacking in force from the southeast. Planes would cross the coast 30nmi northeast of Darwin at the mouth of Adelaide River between Gunn Point and Cape Hotham. After that, a curved flight path of 44nmi allowed each wave to approach its target from the southeast. This path had clear landmarks: the Adelaide River which curved with the flight path, turn before Mt Daly, the Noonmah railway siding with its turning triangle under construction and East Arm which pointed like a sign post to Harbour and Town.

In the first raid, 9 Zeros would attack RAAF Base from the northwest to hold off Kittyhawks as the first wave with 54 Kates attacked Shore and Town from the southeast. On the day, these Zeros had to shoot down a Catalina on the way but made target on time. Because these Zeros had a journey 46nmi shorter than all the other aircraft, they were scheduled to take off with the third wave.

Ten minutes later, in the second raid, 27Kates would attack RAAF Base as 17 Vals supported by 18 Zeros attacked Berrimah and airfield. At this stage 54Vals and 18 Zeros, taking off in two waves, would start the first of three bombing raids on shipping. All raids would attack searchlights, gun emplacements, fuel storage tanks and targets of opportunity.

An hour later, the last wave made up of 27 Nell and 27 Betty bombers would level RAAF Base.

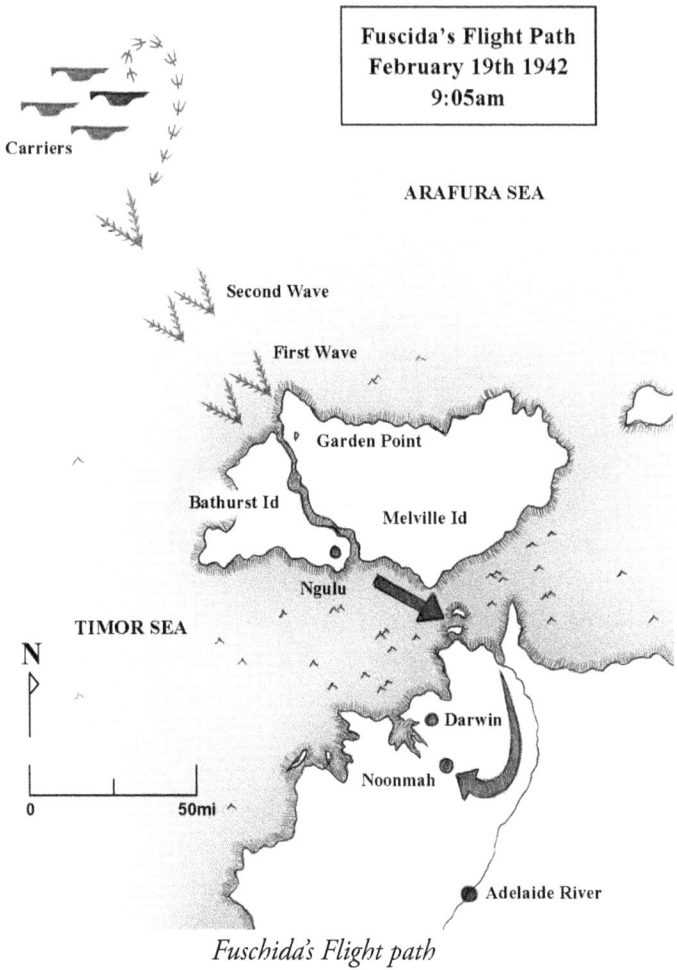

Fuschida's Flight path

This attack was of the same magnitude as that thrown at the relatively vast military assets of Pearl Harbour. Fuschida later said that the Darwin target was "not worthy of Nagumo Force." There was more to this than sinking *Houston*. Many factors may have come together at the same time. Firstly, sinking US Navy Flagship *Houston* would demoralise the Allies bringing honour to the Imperial Japanese Navy and why not make sure by "cracking a nut with a sledgehammer"? Secondly, Nagumo may have lost the argument to take Australia rather than Midway, and this was his chance to prove his point. Thirdly, Imperial Japanese forces, which had already weighed anchor for landings at Koepang and Timor. To be sure of removing Allied assets at Darwin with bombing only, bombing had to be comprehensive. Finally, Japan pursued racial equality at the League of Nations but was blocked by Australian Prime Minister Billy Hughes who was determined that the White Australia Policy remain internationally legal. For this reason Japan had a personal score to settle with Australia and Darwin may have been 'road rage'.

Explanations may be endless.

CHAPTER 7

HOUSTON PLAYS A GHOST TRICK

The *Houston* convoy arrived back in Port Darwin on Wednesday February 18th. *Peary* and *Houston* were quickly re-armed and refuelled, *Peary* detaching into the outer harbour near the convoy transports.

Houston looked as if she were undergoing lengthy repairs on a damaged 8" gun turret which would keep her in port for days. As night fell *Houston* was silhouette camouflaged, her ensigns stored indoors. She ghosted along the bay no faster than a large troop carrier blocked from shore view by *Peary* starboard. It was probably raining.

Together they crossed the gate in the Boom-net, blocked from shore view by *Kangaroo* and *Kara Kara*. Petty Officer 'Nobby' Clark, winch operator on *Kangaroo* watched the pair slip out of port, turn west and set course for Tjilatjap in Java.

Japan's spy was watching from a vantage point near East Point and the silhouettes were telling their lies. Spy reported to the Japanese Flag Ship *Akagi* that *Peary* had departed escorting a transport, the rest of the convoy was in port and *Houston* was damaged and undergoing major repairs.

A Japanese submarine lurking in Beagle Gulf was looking for *Peary* escorting a troop carrier and, like self fulfilling prophesies, confirmed that their spy was correct again.

To achieve sufficient speed to keep up, the submarine had to surface. *Peary* detached to destroy it while *Houston* hurried west. *Peary* hunted into the night frequently travelling at fuel-consuming top speed. The submarine's evasive pattern had an easterly component leading *Peary* back to Darwin at 2:30am on February 19th.

On the other side of Darwin, merchant vessel MV *Don Isidro* was travelling west towards the port on Wednesday February 18th. She had been chartered by the US Army for a blockade run of ammunition and supplies. Her aim was to run, undetected, the Japanese naval blockade of the Philippines with cargo destined for US land forces there.

After the fall of Ceram and The Celebes, routes for approaching the Philippines were drying up. Her Captain Rafael Cisernos was planning to cross the Arafura Sea under the cover of darkness, hug the West New Guinea coastline and approach Corregidor with a night run on the Philippines Sea.

Don Isidro sailed undetected until she left the cover of the Wessel Islands to cross open water to Crocodile Island. By the time she reached Crocodile Island she was being shadowed by a Japanese surveillance aircraft and for a while by a submarine. She was steering as close to the Arnhem Land shoreline as safe navigation would permit, preparing to beach if that proved necessary. At noon, Japanese bombers attacked but she was experienced and evaded the bombs. Cisernos decided to call it off for a while and head for the safety of Port Darwin.

CHAPTER 8
THURSDAY FEBRUARY 19th 1942

7am-9:18am

It was a busy day on hospital ship *Manunda*. Captain James Garden and First Mate Captain Tom Minto were on the bridge. Commanding Officer of the General Hospital, Lieutenant-Colonel John Beith and Matron Clara Jane Shumack RAANS were preparing for 9:30am when they would be in the wards to examine the practical nursing skills of orderlies.

Warrego under Commander Ross V. Wheatley was stationed off Stokes Hill. A detail of sailors was painting the ship while the gunners were closed up at action stations for gunnery drill. Her sister sloop *Swan* was waiting for ammunition from the merchant vessel MV *Neptuna* due to dock before 9am.

It was also a busy day for Lieutenant Commander Ethridge Grant, commander of the American Catalina tender *William B. Preston*. She was one of the tenders belonging to the Tenth Patrol Boat Wing, Patwing 10. Patwing 10 was withdrawing from Ambon via Surabaya to the Swan River Perth. It was becoming a long wait in Darwin and they were a massive target. This was an unacceptable risk for the leader of the squadron, Lieutenant Leroy Deede. Deede left three Patwing 10 Catalinas to wait with the tender in Darwin Harbour as he pressed on to Perth with the rest of the Wing. Also left behind was a Catalina from the second squadron of the second patrol Wing, Patwing 22, a survivor from Hawaii and the Philippines under the command of Lieutenant Tom Moorer.

At 9am Grant took a small motor boat to the wharf near the Signals Station. *William B. Preston* had been queuing for a week to fuel and provision for the journey to Perth. Return of the convoy had pushed her back in the queue again with priority given to *Houston* and *Peary*. Now *Peary* had returned for the second time. Grant wanted early attention as the situation became darker for the Dutch East Indies and he was putting in a personal appearance at Naval Headquarters to press his case.

Preparations were underway for the day's patrolling schedule. Two Catalinas were preparing for patrol duties. One was a Patwing 10 Catalina, which would patrol north, on the lookout for suspected carrier activity. Lieutenant Thomas Moorer and his crew from Patwing 22 were scheduled for the morning patrol on the Arafura Sea sweeping north of the Tiwi Islands looking for suspected Japanese Carriers. Meteorology was encouraging: fine sunny day, 1/8th cumulus cloud cover increasing during the day, no fog, light northwest breeze, calm sea. Moorer looked around the blue sky which sported a few puffs of stationary white cloud in the south. He looked to the northwest, the first leg of his patrol and saw a clear sky darkening at the horizon.

On HMAS *Karangi* gunner Cecil Dobell was greasing the 12lb Ack-Ack and gunner Harry Dale was jotting a few more lines to his mother. When diaries were forbidden for all Allied personnel in Darwin Harry Dale started an endlessly long letter to his mother, which he did not get round to posting.

Zeros takeoff.

At 8.00am, owing to radio transmission failure in a Mavis, reconnaissance of targets and weather over Darwin were not signalled back to Japanese flagship *Akagi*. Their spy in Darwin had already sent a promising weather report and there had been no arrivals or departures since Peary arrived last night. At 8.15am the tides were in place and Nagumo signalled takeoff for 188 aircraft from four carriers: 81 high level Kate bombers, 71 Val dive bombers and 36 Type 'O' Zero fighters.

At 8.55am two camouflaged Patwing Catalinas skimmed northwest across East Arm into the Darwin breeze, lifting gracefully into their morning patrol.

Peary, weary from an all-night submarine chase, anchored at mooring F3 at the entry to East Arm. *Peary* had plenty of ammunition but needed fuel.

It was not long before James Webster, a seventeen year old from Wallasey Cheshire, now a radio operator on the Oiler MV *British Motorist*, radioed *Peary* that the Oiler was coming starboard east of F-3 to anchor 30ft away from *Peary* and start refuelling. This location was significant because *British Motorist* would be shielding both *Peary* and MV *Zealandia* during any attack from the southeast. *Zealandia* was next in line for wharf access, having arrived in Darwin under escort on February 6th. On this information the Wharf was running a fortnight late.

British Motorist was built by Swan Hunter and Wigham Richardson at Newcastle-on-Tyne for the British Tanker Company in 1924. With a crew of 61 British merchant seamen she was now on charter to the US Asia Fleet carrying oil, aviation fuel and petrol for army vehicles. The commander of *Peary*, Lieutenant Commander J.M. Bermingham watched while the Master of *British Motorist*, Gilbert C. Bates, controlled the operation.

Oilers of this class delivered fuel via a hose strung between the vessels. The typical delivery rate was 5gal/sec and the fuel capacity of a destroyer around 750t. Given that *Peary's* fuel level was about 40% it was going to take around 5 hours to top her up.

Six unannounced Hudson Bombers of No 2 Squadron from Penfoi approached from the northwest over Melville

Island at 7am. They were too high for Coastwatcher John Gribble to identify but these aircraft were not using the 'friendly' route inbound. As required of him under these circumstances Gribble signalled Warrant Officer Bill Phaup at HMAS *Coonawarra* who telephoned Naval Intelligence staff officer Lieutenant Commander JCB McManus who telephoned RAAF Intelligence who were reluctant to pass it on to Area Combined Headquarters because there had been many such signals, all false alarms and Wing Commander Sturt Griffith, the man with his hand on the air raid sirens, was not going to be ridiculed again. RAAF Intelligence passed it on to the Operations Controller Flight Lieutenant CG Fenton who discussed it with Griffith. Fenton telephoned on the dedicated line to the Experimental Radar Station at Dripstone Caves and asked for a count on the number of approaching planes. The Radar Officer told him that the radar would soon be up but could not be used at the moment. Together, Fenton and Griffith monitored the situation and soon realised it was a false alarm. The planes took so long to reach the Darwin defence perimeter that they had to be friendly because Japanese planes did not travel that slowly. Sergeant Laurie Huby at the 2/14th Fannie Bay AA emplacement put up a salvo as a warning to the Hudsons to approach identified.

At Darwin RAAF Base a B-17E Flying Fortress had been waiting around since 6:30am ready to do navigational duty for the ten Kittyhawks of Pursuit Squadron 17 (Provisional) scheduled to take off at dawn. The flight was held up by engine and radio problems until 9am when at last the B-17E took off followed by the Kittyhawks in two flights of five. The first, called flight 'A' was led by Major Floyd Pell and the second, flight 'B' was led by Lieutenant Robert Oesteicher. They cleared the airport turning west and the duty officer watched them getting smaller and smaller against the western sky. Their destination was Java refuelling at Koepang in Timor and Denpasar in Bali. The departure was observed by Griffith and Fenton.

At Pirlangimpi (Garden Point) on the northwest coast of Melville Island Navy Reserve Coastwatcher Lieutenant John Gribble had been expressing his disenchantment with officers at the various headquarters he was trying to serve. Brother Edward Bennett thought John might need a friend and was sitting with him at the Coastwatcher post around 9am. With the Japanese taking Allied Bases in the islands to the north there was a lot of air traffic retreating to Darwin unannounced. His warnings had caused headquarters to sound the Darwin air raid sirens quite often and they were starting to blame him for the false alarms. Wing Commander Sturt Griffith had sounded the false alarms from Area Combined Headquarters and was equally disenchanted with his senior officer, Group Captain Frederick Scherger, who, albeit jokingly, may have announced in front of the men that Griffith was becoming 'the boy who cried wolf'. Griffith projected this on to Gribble.

Gribble knew that headquarters ignored a warning which he sent at 7am that morning. When aircraft fly too high or too far away to identify wing markings or silhouette shapes, a spotter can only estimate their altitude, strength and bearing. It was up to Operations to identify the aircraft.

As far as John was concerned from now on they could shove it up their kilt. As Brother Bennett tried to console John and help him towards grace, John grabbed the binoculars and focussed 5nmi out to sea. He noted the time, 9.06am and told Brother Bennett that the aircraft were too high to identify but there were about 60 of them at 25,000ft heading southeast.

As the planes passed overhead Brother Bennett asked John why he wasn't reporting it. John could see no point in doing so. The shiny-bums at headquarters would ignore it anyhow. The Brother insisted. John fobbed him off saying he didn't have the necessary code books. The Brother protested, went to report it himself on Aeradio only to find, on his own recollection later, no one listening. What John had observed was the first wave of the attack. There were 54 Kates at 25,000ft and no escort Zeros.

The Royal Australian Navy had a long range naval wireless station at HMAS *Coonawarra* in the Darwin suburb of Berrimah. According to the log book, at 9:15am, Lieutenant John Gribble, Navy Reserve Coastwatcher on Melville Island radioed Coonawarra and reported "a large number of aircraft bearing southeast." What Gribble saw at 9:15am was the second wave with 27 Kates at 25,000ft followed by 17 Vals at 20,000ft escorted by 9 Zeros at similar altitude, in all, 53 aircraft. John got the wind up when he saw the second wave because he knew that in the space of ten minutes he had seen over 100 aircraft heading towards Darwin and hadn't reported at the first opportunity. Three of the Zeros were sent to strafe the source of the message. The pilots couldn't see Gribble's hideout but were flying so low that Brother Bennett later said "I could see the heads of the pilots they were so low."

Gribble's message was received by Warrant Officer Bill Phaup at HMAS *Coonawarra*. Within minutes Phaup telephoned McManus who telephoned the RAAF Intelligence Officer. There followed a conversation where RAAF Intelligence challenged the claim and McManus would not have it rejected. RAAF Intelligence did not pass it on to Flight Lieutenant Fenton at RAAF Operations. The testimonies of officers named in this paragraph were omitted from the Lowe Royal Commission Report losing all substantiation of Gribble's message. Until now, the question has been whether or not Gribble reported. When Peter and Sheila Forrest interviewed Brother Edward Bennett he testified to them that he was *with Gribble that day and Gribble did not send the message*. Historians and writers believed the priest concluding that Gribble did not report. As this new story line shows, Gribble did not report the first wave of Japanese bombers when Bennett was with him but reported the second wave ten minutes later after Bennett had left him. No doubt the priest heard or saw the second wave and seems to have presumed that Gribble still wasn't reporting.

9.19am

At the Roman Catholic Mission Station at Nguiu, Father John McGrath heard the drone of high flying aircraft. He looked at his watch as these aircraft appeared overhead just east of him. It was nearly twenty past nine.

He got that 'Pearl Harbour feeling' but it took him over

fifteen minutes to get to his radio shack. He radioed, "Eight to VID, big flight of planes passed over going south very high over." Lou Curnock, an avid log book keeper at the AWA coastal station VID recorded that McGrath's message was received at 9:35am. At 9:37am Curnock telephoned directly to Pilot Officer Saxton at RAAF Operations to report "an unusually large air formation bearing down on us from the northwest, identity suspect, visibility not clear." Saxton passed the message on directly to Fenton who discussed it with Griffith.

The priest went outside to watch further waves passing over when, suddenly, like a bolt from the blue, three Zeros strafed his radio shack. The Japanese now had the frequency of the radio and it would only be a matter of time before they could start jamming. McGrath's message confirmed that he was reporting the first wave "very high". The angry Zeros were with the second or third waves 10 and 17 minutes later. This confirms that McGrath took some little time to get to his radio.

Nguiu is 27nmi southeast of Garden Point. McGrath was at Nguiu and Gribble was at Garden Point. McGrath reported these aircraft overhead at 9.19am, four minutes after Gribble at 9.15am. If they were seeing the same flight of aircraft, Gribble 5nmi offshore, McGrath overhead, the flight travelled 32nmi in 4 minutes requiring a speed of 480kn. The maximum speed of Kates and Vals was 205kn and that of Zeros 287kn. It is thus revealed that McGrath reported the first wave and Gribble reported the second wave. This is probably the first forensic analysis of the data, previous accounts of the Battle tacitly assuming that

Gribble and McGrath saw the same formation of planes. It may also explain testimonies dropped from the Lowe Royal Commission Report.

While Zero pilots were looking for the source of McGrath's message they spotted *Don Isidro*. Zeros strafed her decks, several were wounded and all her life boats were rendered useless. At the time of the attack Don Isidro was off the southeast coast of Bathurst Island. Since his main defence after the attack was to avoid further detection, Captain Rafael Cisernos headed for the western side of Bathurst Island. His ship was capable of 20kn and he made the most of it. 'Don's Zeros', as we will call them, had to step on the gas to catch up with their wave of Vals.

9.20am-9.58am

At 9:19am Captain Louis J. Connelly from Army Air Corp Operations radioed Pell to advise that there was cloud down to 600ft over southern Timor with scattered heavy rainstorms and the meteorology was not likely to change before Pell reached Penfoi. Pell knew that on Tuesday, February 10th, the United States Army Air Corp 3rd pursuit squadron, navigated by an LB-30 Liberator, flew from Darwin to Koepang. The weather conditions over Timor for that flight were similar to those awaiting his squadron. The Liberator eventually found the airfield. In the meantime, the eight Kittyhawks which were flown by pilots as inexperienced as Pell's pilots, ran out of fuel and all crashed.

At 9.20am Pell detached from the B-17E and returned to Darwin. The B-17E continued to Timor. At 9.40am Pell's Flight A was landing unannounced at RAAF Base while

Oestreicher's Flight B started to patrol east in the Darwin defence zone. Pell and Oestreicher were unaware that Japanese bombers were about to cross the coast 32nmi to the northeast.

Tom Moorer's Catalina patrol was off the northwest corner of Bathurst Island. At 9:30am Moorer spotted a ship and identified it as MV *Florence D.* Like *Don Isidro, Florence D.* had been chartered by the US army for a blockade run of the Philippines. Her cargo included 200,000 rounds of ammunition.

In a surprise attack at 9:35am nine zeros in the last wave pounced on the Catalina. Moorer's gunner defended while Moorer tried to signal the attack. At 9:37am Zeros unleashed a spray of machine gun fire that injured four of the crew, tore the port engine away from its housing, ripped open its fuselage and holed a fuel tank starting a fire. Moorer crash landed, the whole crew climbing into the life raft before the Catalina sank. The crew of *Florence D.* who witnessed the fight from a distance set course to pick up survivors. After this delay, 'Moorer's Zeros' as we will call them, increased speed to 260kn and set course for RAAF Base to attack from the northwest, as planned, just before bombers arrived over Darwin from the southeast.

Moorer's signal arrived at *William B. Preston* and she came to full alert. It was also received by Bill Phaup who recorded it in the *Coonawarra* logbook at 9:37am. The message was passed on quickly through the channels and arrived with Flight Lieutenant Fenton by 9:45am. Realising the negative psychological effect Scherger had on

Griffith, Fenton, as officers in his position do, suggested that Scherger join the conversation. Scherger was off Base, not to be disturbed for the rest of the day and preferred not to delegate his authority to Griffith even for one day.

As they had done at 7am, Griffith and Fenton searched the northwest sky for incoming aircraft. Even if the sirens were sounded when aircraft reached the Darwin perimeter that would give some warning and a false alarm avoided. McGrath was 56nmi to the north and, if he saw Japanese aircraft, these planes would appear in the northwest at the same time as Pell's Kittyhawks were landing. Fenton rang the Experimental Radar Station at Dripstone Caves to get a count on the approaching aircraft. The line was dead. It was 9:45am and the Kittyhawks were landing at the same time as the incoming planes were expected. They considered the possibility that McGrath saw the Kittyhawks. This was always a ludicrous conclusion given that the Kittyhawks were always over McGrath's southern horizon travelling west when McGrath reported planes above him travelling south. By 9:50am the pressure was off. It was the same as it was between 7am and 8am. The incoming planes were friendly because Japanese planes did not fly that slowly. It was probably more Hudsons which would arrive in the next few minutes. When they didn't, Fenton and Griffith kept looking northwest. Now it was clear that McGrath must have seen eleven fast travelling Kittyhawks. As for Moorer, he obviously got caught in a skirmish with a Japanese patrol and Coonawarra had already raised a rescue signal on HMAS *Warnambool*.

Fuschida completely fooled them.

The RAAF officers decided that the incoming aircraft were the Kittyhawks and did not issue warnings. For RAAF Base, Navy, Merchant Marine and Air Raid Precautions a chance to make last minute preparations had slipped away. There were 70 Wharfies on day shift when the bombing started at 9:58am. Even 5 minutes warning would have given them a chance to shelter on shore. The warning was withheld, 22 Wharfies were killed or drowned immediately and 48 were injured. Townsfolk were out of doors looking up at the planes as the first bombs fell.

RAAF Base Commander Sturt Griffith withheld the warning. Group Captain Frederick Scherger provided Griffith's motive, avoidance of further ridicule; Fuschida provided his opportunity by not having bombers approach from the northwest; and Franklin D. Roosevelt, who sent 10 Kittyhawks, provided Griffith with the means to withhold the siren. The Lowe Royal Commission held Scherger responsible.

Australian Command had failed to bring defences to a state of readiness in the face of a clear and present threat. The RAAF had ignored a timely warning of the approach of a large formation of unidentified aircraft. In short, Australian military leadership at home had learnt nothing from the attacks on Pearl Harbour and Singapore.

CHAPTER 9
ZERO v KITTYHAWK
FIRST ATTACK ON RAAF BASE

Kittyhawk Flight A under Major Floyd Pell had landed unannounced at RAAF Base while Flight B under Lieutenant Robert Oestreicher was climbing east off Gunn Point on protective patrol.

"Don's Zeros" set course to rendezvous with their Vals. At 9.46am they were at 12,000ft approaching the Japanese main flight off Gunn Point when they unexpectedly spotted Oestreicher's Flight B Kittyhawks below them at 2 o'clock. They called the 18 escorting Zeros in the third wave to stand by at 20,000ft and attacked the Kittyhawks.

Lieutenant Robert Oestreicher USAAC and his Kittyhawk

The Zero was a fast, manoeuvrable fighter, superior to the Kittyhawk except at low altitude. To achieve its performance the Zero, unlike the Kittyhawk was designed with no armour plating and no self-sealing fuel tank. It was thus vulnerable to ground attack but dangerous against enemy fighters particularly at higher altitude.

A key factor was pilot experience. The Japanese pilots had chalked up hundreds of flying hours and were seasoned from Manchuria, China, Pearl Harbour and the Philippines. In contrast, Lieutenant Robert G. Oestreicher was the only pilot in the American patrol with more than 20 hours flying time and none had fired in anger. Oestreicher was flying 'weaver' at 10,000ft, turning and rotating 2,000ft above the other four Kittyhawks looking for enemy threats, his radio handy in case he had to warn them.

"Zero, Zero, Zero! 8 o'clock high," called Oestreicher dropping his belly tank to pick up speed. He watched the first Zero "barge" through breaking up the Kittyhawk formation. As a natural evasive reaction, three Kittyhawks dived south towards the coast. With numbers, surprise, experience and superior aircraft on their side, the Japanese rapidly shot down two of the three Kittyhawks. Lieutenant Elton S Perry and Lieutenant Jack Peres were killed instantly.

On the ground, the air battle was seen by Corporal Ted Campbell and other soldiers of the 2/14th Heavy Anti Aircraft Battery. The men reported their sighting immediately but their officers thought the men were 'leg-pulling', and were determined not to look like fools to the General. Notwithstanding this reaction from some officers, eves droppers on the telephone network in Darwin, like the telephonist at the 2/14th AA on the Oval, were hearing excited messages like "dogfight out at sea".

Corporal Edwin Campbell
2/14th AA Battery

Around 9.46am Major R.B. Hone telephoned RAAF from the 2/14th at Nightcliffe to report a sighting of a P-40E (Kittyhawk) and parachute. RAAF scolded him for trying to make out that this event could be called a raid. At 9.50am Hone reported a dog fight off Nightcliffe to Army Headquarters but no further action was taken. At the 19th Machine Gun Post at Casuarina Beach Trooper Cecil Burns reported a sighting of aircraft to Sergeant W.J.F. McDonald who reported it to Captain Howard Brown at 23rd Brigade Headquarters. Brown said he was busy, not to play games with him and asked McDonald how he knew the planes were Japs? McDonald said he thought they were Japs because there were so many of them.

Back in the sky a Zero shooting at Lieutenant William Walker's Kittyhawk wounded him in the shoulder. The Zero pilots could see Walker's blood splattering on the cockpit and left him to it. Walker veered away looking for

RAAF Base, the Zero pilots missing their last chance to kill Walker, who would live to tell the tale.

The radio in Lieutenant Max Wiecks' Kittyhawk was out of order so he did not hear Oestreicher's warning. His lack of response surprised the Zero pilots but one Zero looped, rolled and shot Wiecks' plane to shreds. Wiecks was superficially injured and parachuted into the sea about 8nmi off the coast. With his eyes at water level he could not see land but started to swim with the sun behind him on the left. The tide fell over 20ft that day and carried him further out to sea. He continued to swim shoreward resting periodically in his Mae-West. At 2.19pm the tide turned and brought him ashore after dark. He sat on the beach to recover his strength and watched the moon set.

Oestreicher was the pilot of the remaining Kitty Hawk. He climbed into the sun. A Zero appeared in his sights and he hit it with a burst of machine gun fire as he climbed. The pilot of the Zero rolled, raked Oestreicher's wing, nicked the tyre on one of his landing wheels but the armour plating on the Kittyhawk prevented further damage. Oestreicher spun out regaining control at 4,000ft, using his speed to ascend steeply at 50 feet per second, dropping back naturally to 35 feet per second. This may have been the start of a dogfight strategy called 'the yo-yo' but at 12,000ft Oestreicher counted "18 more enemy planes in a lazy circle" which he judged to be at 20,000ft. He changed tactics and headed for long white cumulus cloud cover at 2,500ft. His call for Flight B to follow was to ears that couldn't hear him. The cloud cover was parallel to the coast, five miles inland. When the opportunity presented, Oestreicher climbed to 20,000ft to hover, as hawks do, on the aerial highway.

It was now 9:55am and Oestreicher reached for his radio to call in the bomber attack with the important fact that it was all happening east of and out of sight of Town, Harbour and RAAF Base. Pell received the message. He had also received Oestreicher's earlier message, "Zeros!" and was urgently recalling his pilots to scramble. The RAAF duty officers were no doubt viewing Pell's activity as a response to a skirmish not an invasion.

'Moorer's Zeros' arrived from the northwest at 9.56am to attack the Boom Defence of Darwin. At that moment minesweeper HMAS Gunbar, on duty as Water Carrier under Lieutenant Commander Norman N. Muzzel was passing through the Boom Gate. The Zeros caught her crew by surprise with a mix of armour piercing, tracer and .303. Gunbar was the first Allied ship attacked in the Battle of Darwin. Ordinary Seaman Herbert J. Shepherd was wounded mortally and eight others were injured, including Muzzel in both legs. Gunbar's Vickers machine gun could not elevate much above horizontal so it mattered little that the Zeros had knocked it out. Marksmen led by Master at Arms Henry Lucas opened fire with their single shot Lee-Enfield .303 rifles, the wounded Muzzel with his Webley service revolver. As the attackers raced over them, Muzzel yelled to his men, "Our fire is like throwing peanuts at a tiger."

Gunbar entered port at top speed, 10kn, because she had no radio and had to report the attack using the *Kara Kara* radio. There she paused to evacuate five of her wounded in a lifeboat to Manunda. Kara Kara with a crew of 39 had been strafed as well, injuring Petty Officer Frank Moore and the cook, Fred Emms. Emms and Moore joined the *Gunbar* lifeboat en route to *Manunda*.

As Moorer's Zeros wheeled east from Boom-net to RAAF Base at 9.58am, 54 Kate bombers were starting their first bombing run across Darwin's Shore and Town. The first attack was spot on time, nine Zeros to remove the threat of Allied fighters at RAAF Base and 54 Kates to take out strategic targets along Darwin's Town and Shoreline.

One of Moorer's Zeros detached briefly to strafe a chauffeur-driven staff car heading towards town down Bagot Road. The chauffeur was caught by surprise but his reflex action was just in time. The senior officer in the car was Group Captain Frederick Scherger on his way to town for a secret appointment with Air Vice-Marshall Sir Richard Williams. Scherger jumped out of his car, took cover and looked around. He realised quickly that he had been a target of convenience for a fighter, that a major air offensive was in progress and he ordered the chauffeur to drive back to RAAF Base only to find vehicles blocking the gate.

The five Kitty Hawks at RAAF Base were still fuelled, fully armed and their engines were warm. The pilots raced back to their aircraft and quickly prepared. The wheels on Robert McMahon's Kittyhawk were jammed in the down-position but there was no time for undercarriage adjustments.

As Major Floyd Pell started to take off, his Kitty Hawk was

strafed by three Zeros and caught fire. Pell parachuted out but his altitude was less than 80 feet. His chute opened, substantially broke his fall and he started to drag himself to safety. One of the attackers returned and strafed him to death.

Lieutenant Charles Hughs died instantly at take-off when a Zero using heavy fire turned Hughs' Kittyhawk into a fire ball which continued briefly into the air then rolled over and over beside the runway. Ironically, this provided a diversion while the other three pilots took off.

Lieutenant Robert McMahon was half way down the runway lifting off when Lieutenant William Walker crossed in front of him. Walker, his shoulder bleeding profusely from the air battle over Gunn Point, taxied well off the strip away from buildings. Walker slumped into a slit trench and saw a Zero strafe his plane.

McMahon climbed towards the sun with his Kittyhawk's landing wheels locked in the down-position. He turned left and flew down Frances Bay where smoke and fire were bellowing from the oil tank farm on his right and Kates in the first wave were bombing the inner port, shore and town from 26,000ft. He flew across the port in the direction of Mission Point. Below him, the machine gunners on *Admiral Halstead* had been holding fire because their guns weren't capable above 9000ft. Suddenly they saw a low flying plane coming at them from the north. Its wheels were permanently down, a sure sign of a Japanese Val dive bomber. At one and the same time, McMahon came under friendly fire, suffered speed reduction from the drag on his landing gear and three Zeros were 'up his arse'.

As the Australian cricketer Keith Miller would say, "That's pressure!"

McMahon engaged three Zeros in a dog fight. He was about to lose when his luck changed. Edward Johnson, Master of *Admiral Halstead* and leader of the machine gun crew recognised the wing stars on McMahon's Kittyhawk. He redirected the ship's machine gun fire at the Zeros which broke up their coordination and forced them away from McMahon. The Zeros suddenly flew off in the direction of the civil aerodrome to support 17 Val bombers about to attack that target. They were quickly replaced by nine Zeros, fully stocked with ammunition, escorting 27 Val bombers into their first attack across the Harbour.

Aichi D3A 'Val' dive bomber attacking

Two Val dive bombers, working as a pair, attacked *Admiral Halstead* from the stern. Johnson was determined to spare his cargo of 14,000 drums of aviation gasoline and petrol for Army vehicles but the Vals were attacking from different directions to halve the intensity of his machine gun fire. He was about to split his fire when his luck changed. McMahon's Kittyhawk did a half roll pointing its nose at one Val and began shooting tracer at it, leaving Johnson, who could see the tracer, at full fire power on the other Val. After McMahon attacked, he saw the rear gunner in the Val slump over his gun. A Zero attacked McMahon's Kittyhawk forcing him to take cover in nearby cloud. With his ammunition depleted McMahon was inevitably shot down and parachuted into mangroves on the western side of the harbour.

Bleeding and up to his calves in mud McMahon climbed a tree to attract rescuers but all he could see was a battle raging in the port and a couple of small crocodiles camouflaged on a muddy beach, their dinosaur mouths half open and completely still. He strapped a compress on his injured leg to stop the flow of blood and sat on his parachute seat in the water slapping its surface in the belief that this would scare off crocodiles. The forked channels of West Arm were ebbing quickly creating a current that swept him towards middle arm as he yelled for help. Nearby, a rescuer looking for him had mercifully cut the engine of his launch to listen.

Lieutenant Burt Rice had taken off with Lieutenant John Glover close behind, both Kittyhawks taking strafe damage. Rice climbed to 5000ft when suddenly his controls failed to respond throwing him forward. Rice bumped his head causing concussion. By instinct, he bailed out and pulled the rip cord. The Japanese pilots tried to strafe him in the air as he descended but were foiled by John Glover who abandoned his climb and fired straight at the Zeros breaking up their formation. Glover thought he hit one of the Zeros drawing smoke near its cockpit. He circled and shielded Rice in his parachute down to 3000ft when his own Kittyhawk suddenly fell into a dive. He levelled out but his plane cart-wheeled across the airfield. Miraculously, Glover crawled out from under the wreckage and started to walk down the strip. An Australian helped him to safety while Glover scanned the sky for the Zero he might have shot down. All he could see were Zeros heading for the Civil Airport and getting away from RAAF Base.

Rice survived. He landed in a swamp and was found hours later.

CHAPTER 10
KATES OVER TOWN AND SHORE

While the air battle was raging in the eastern skies between Kittyhawk Flight B and Don's Zeros, *Swan* attached starboard to *Neptuna* which was moored on the outer berth of the main jetty at Stokes Hill wharf.

A crew of 70 wharfies was at work and some had started to unload Neptuna by opening Hatches 1, 3 and 4. The commander of *Swan*, Lieutenant Alan J Travis needed fuel and ammunition after returning from the *Houston* Convoy. On an understanding with William Michie, Master of *Neptuna*, Travis secured Swan alongside so that RAN sailors could board *Neptuna* and transfer anti-aircraft ammunition directly. This was detected by the wharfies who sent their shop steward backed up by their two biggest wharfies, Col and Toby Giles, to confront the petty officer of *Swan*. The shop steward's case was that the ammunition, being general cargo had to be unloaded and reloaded by wharfies and that RAN sailors should cease work immediately or else he'd call a strike. The Petty Officer's case, backed up by all the seamen and sailors was that the wharfies were too slow and should get back to work before they were 'thrown in the drink'.

9:58am to 10:08 am

Some 54 high altitude bombers called Kates, assigned to destroy shore and town facilities, approached from the southeast along East Arm in saturation bombing formations.

Their targets lined up from wharf and oil farm at one end, through Town to military Barracks at the other end.

At 9.55am, three minutes before the attack, experienced lookouts on the battle-hardened *William B. Preston* called down, "large formations of planes approaching from the southeast." Lieutenant Lester O. Wood, standing in for Ethridge Grant who had gone ashore, called *battle stations* and the flying boat tender was underway before the Kate attack started. Her Catalinas were left to fend for themselves. Wood was pleased with his experienced lookouts: if Japanese planes were coming they would be expected from the northwest. His responsibility was to get out of East Arm, weave through the crowded harbour to the Boom Gate and head for the open sea. His sense of urgency was driven by William B. Preston's cargo of 50X500lb bombs and 30,000gal of aviation gasoline. This cargo was the reason why one boiler was always kept going for a fast getaway, why her 9X0.5in and 5X0.30in anti-aircraft machine guns were kept loaded and her radio was always attended for messages from her patrolling Catalinas. She had two patrolling: one of her Patwing-22 Catalinas was patrolling north between the Timor and Arafura Seas looking for Japanese carriers and Tom Moorer who signalled he was under attack at 9:37am.

Warrego was anchored northwest of *William B. Preston* at the mouth of Frances Bay with a clear view down East Arm. On *Warrego* the gunnery drill had used west-bound Kittyhawks to simulate a target at 9.05am and again on their return about 9:40 am. The lookouts identified the incoming Kates and even before the alarm sounded the guns changed to live ammunition and the crew to action stations. *Warrego* was the first ship to open fire and won the Naval Battle Honour for Darwin 1942.

The commercial Flying Boat Base in Darwin was located in Frances Bay next to the Oil Tank Farm at Stokes Hill. William Wake, OIC of the base, had one Flying boat VH-ADU 'Camilla' at anchor. The Department of Civil Aviation (DCA) used shuttle tenders to ferry passengers to and from the anchored Flying boats and the officers on duty were Lieutenant Ian McRoberts and coxswain John Waldie. McRoberts and Waldie heard the Kates coming. The shuttle tenders and DCA depot were stationary targets. As soon as bombing started Waldie called a boat hand to join him and headed for open water in tender CA22. Soon after, McRoberts had tender C2 on the move.

On *Karangi* gunner Harry Dale later wrote that at 9:57am he saw planes at 30,000ft glistening silver in the Sun flying in a giant arrow head formation, with one leader, ready to pattern bomb. He asked gunner Cecil Dobell if these might be friendly planes. Dobell said "They're Japs, we don't own that many." As Dale hit the alarm button he saw planes over Darwin Town dropping their bombs simultaneously. *Karangi* made steam. Her anchor was on a stanchion and the chain slipped quickly to the bottom of the harbour. She was away. Her 12lb AA guns were not capable above 12,000ft. The gunners estimated Kates at 30,000ft, withheld fire and waited to start evasive tactics.

As Kates began their first bombing run, a sailor on *Swan* pointed skywards over Darwin Town. "At last the Yanks have arrived!" he yelled. As everyone looked up, a seaman from *Neptuna* responded, "Look, they're dropping leaflets."

HMAS *Platypus* was a submarine tender permanently anchored off Stokes Hill. Channel Patrol Lugger *Mavie* was tied to her amidships. The *Platypus* klaxon wailed across the harbour. The Town air raid sirens joined in but were quickly drowned out by the fearful whistle of falling bombs.

The demarcation dispute on the wharf informally adjourned. Shop steward and other wharfies including Col and Toby Giles scurried for shelter. RAN sailors transferring ammunition from *Neptuna* swarmed back on to *Swan*.

A cluster of bombs struck the oil tank farm at Stokes Hill hitting tanks and puncturing oil pipes running out along the wharf. The 18th Field Regiment protecting the farm opened fire briefly with their light machine guns which were incapable against high altitude aircraft.

The first pattern of bombs, splitting, splintering and shattering the huge hardwood planks, sliced off a seventy foot section of the wharf on the landward side. An 800kg bomb struck the turntable at the same time as Col was crossing it, with Toby running ahead on the wharf and further to the left. It was a direct hit on Col. Col disappeared and nineteen others around him were dissected instantly. It amputated Toby's leg as it flung him into the harbour but he survived.

Manunda was anchored off Fort Hill close to the northern side of the wide main channel. The leading Kate seen by Harry Dale was Fuschida's. He was leading the attack today even as he did ten weeks earlier at Pearl Harbour calling, "Tora! Tora! Tora!" After the attack on Pearl Harbour, Emperor Hirohito called Fuschida to Tokyo for a grilling. Japan was a signatory to the Geneva Convention guaranteeing immunity to hospitals, hospital ships, ships of Mercy and all other places carrying the Red Cross. The Emperor took this very seriously as a matter of honour for Japan. The Emperor left Fuschida in no doubt. Attacks on hospitals were an act of dishonour for Emperor and Japan and would not be tolerated. Fuschida reassured him that this message was made loud and clear to all pilots before all raids. Fuschida saw the Red Cross on *Manunda's* funnel but she was not in his attack corridor and could not be taken accidentally by this Passover.

Around the shore fire-on-oil was creeping out along the wharf and oil-on-fire into the port. Blazing fuel oil raced across the water engulfing men and rescue boats. With no hope of escaping to land via the pier, wharfies and seamen were starting to jump into the water. The oil, less dense, floated on top of the sea water reducing the buoyancy for survivors trying to keep their heads in a breathing position. The surface tensions of burning oil and sea water configured slicks and patches that threatened survivors struggling to keep out of harm's way. To make matters worse, a 22ft tide had peaked before 8am and now it was ebbing at nearly 3kn carrying burning oil and survivors with it.

Zealandia had been one of the evacuation ships taking civilians to Sydney and returning back-loaded with troops and equipment, on this occasion an anti tank company with weapons and ammunition. The crew was doing lifeboat drills at the time of the attack. How convenient that proved to be with volunteers quickly taking lifeboats to pick up survivors amongst the human and physical debris on the burning water.

Swan cast lines from *Neptuna* and manoeuvred full astern, her anti aircraft guns at the ready. *Neptuna* was showered with debris, some of it burning, but the Kate's near misses left her with light damage only. Her mobility had been limited by work in progress to replace the pistons in her port engine but now it was limited by the time it would take to restore steam to her starboard engine.

HMAS *Katoomba* was locked in the floating dry dock and there she would be for the duration, a stationary target. Her Captain A.P. Cousins, DSO RANR, was savvy. His stock of depth charges was his greatest risk of calamity. He had these weapons set to 'safe', lowered to the bottom of the dock and rolled as far away from the ship as possible. Cousins knew that *Katoomba's* high altitude anti-aircraft 12pounder was not capable at the altitude of the Kates. He was already aware of Japanese tactics, brought his Vickers machine guns and rifles to the ready on both sides of the ship and trotted out 40mm Bofors and ammunition which he had picked up along the way.

The convoy transports: *Port Mar, Mauna Loa, Meigs* and *Tulagi* had returned to a clogged harbour and were waiting to offload troops and equipment. Furthest from the wharf, these ships were moored in an arc around the west side of the port in line with *Admiral Halstead*, Supply Hulk *Kelat* and SS *Benjamin Franklin*. On Tulagi Sergeant Merrill Hulse and Private Roylie Sam of the Idaho 148th Field Regiment led a team bringing their heavy machine guns up on deck to reinforce the ship's light machine guns. By then the Kates were gone and the US gunners sat pat.

The corvette HMAS *Deloraine* was anchored at the buoy closest to *Neptuna* and near the Oil Tank Farm. Her boilers had been dismantled for overhaul making her a stationary target. Projectiles from nearby bomb blasts and heat radiating from the oil fires left her scorched but superficially damaged.

On *Manunda* boson Gus Hampton went below to help the ship's electrician O'Malley to abandon his routine maintenance on the backup generator, reassemble and test forthwith. The hospital might need it sooner rather than later. On *Manunda* the practical nursing examination for orderlies had suddenly become 'no duff'. Captain Minto was launching lifeboats to pick up survivors and bring the wounded back to the ship from sea and shore. One of the lifeboats was lowered but kept on the winch to act as an elevator conveying the wounded on board from rescue boats.

Town targets were strategic. The sea cable from Europe was connected to the Overland Telegraph Cable at Darwin linking Australia to the world. The Post Master was Hurtle Bald. His staff members were his wife Alice, their daughter Iris and seven others.

Fannie Bay

A Oil Tank Farm
B DCA Flying Boat
C Rlwy Station
D China Town
E Court
F Police Admin
G GPO
H Overland Tele
I Govt Hse
J Admiralty
K Hotel
L AA Battery
M AA Quarters
N School
O Aeradio VID
P New Hosp
Q Army Barracks
R Boom Jetty
S Main Wharf

What Japanese Bomber Crews saw
approaching Town from the Southeast

Lighter
SS *Barossa*
SS *Neptuna*
HMAS *Swan*

Darwin Shore and Town

As planes appeared over the harbour, people in Town could hear and see them coming. Because there were no air raid warnings they thought it was safe to come out of doors to look. It was Public Service payday and everyone felt in high spirits. In Town the first notice of an air raid was the terrifying sound of falling bombs at 9:58am. The on-shore air raid sirens were late. Pattern bombing was taking out strategic infrastructure as quickly as possible.

Miss Daisy Martin, a mixed race girl who served as a kitchen maid at Government House sheltered with the Administrator's family in the main house. Three bombs struck, one a direct hit on the house with masonry collapsing into Daisy's place of shelter. Administrator Aubrey Abbott became occupied with securing Government House china and wine cellar from looters and overlooked trying to rescue Miss Martin or trying to assess her condition. She was at least partially crushed and was dead by the time she was dug out after the attack.

One pattern of bombs hit Government House, the Post Master General's post office, telegraph office, cable office and the submarine cable from Java. At this stage Japan had succeeded in cutting communications between Australia and the world. Postmaster Bald could hear a bomb coming and was grateful that his family and staff had already made it to their slit trench. As he ran from the building to join them he was followed by telephone mechanic Reginald Rattley who thought the trench too crowded and headed for the Esplanade cliff. Rattley could hear a bomb coming and had to escape by jumping from the high cliff. He thought it a miracle that the blast pressure opposed his fall giving him a soft landing on the beach. He must have used up all the luck because the 250kg bomb which Bald was hearing fell directly into his slit trench killing all therein. The following bomb was a direct hit on the Post Office and residence. Another pattern of bombs exploded all at once taking out the Court House, Police Station, Police Barracks, Administrator's Office, Government Offices and the Darwin Telephone Exchange. All telephone lines went dead.

The town centre was shattered and rocked by the blast of 800kg bombs. Kates bombed commercial shops and buildings. Saturation bombing reduced the Town to ruins, knocked out the transmission pylons and high voltage lines from the power stations at Stuart Park, directly hit elevated water storage tanks and destroyed rows of private residences.

This was a Blitz!

Military installations and gun emplacements around the town were shattered. Bombs hit the oval spraying AA gunners of the 2/14th with rock and dirt blasted over their revetment walls. Simultaneously bombs struck their quarters north of the oval causing extensive damage. The Oval Group's 4 HA 3.7inch 28pounder guns were capable of 29,500ft with a horizontal range of 11.7mi but gunners were struggling to tune their fuse setter equipment. Their salvos were exploding short at 14,000ft and well in the wake of their targets. Heavy AA was the only gun capable against Kates but the fuse times had not been adjusted for tropical heat and this was the first time firing in anger.

At the end of the bombing run was the Larrakeyah Military Barracks on the south side of Cullen Bay. The Barracks were well camouflaged and the Kate bombardier was looking through a telescope with a limited field of view from 27,000ft. The bombs fell short, two landing near the new Darwin Hospital damaging it physically and functionally. The Hospital buildings were not camouflaged and a key question, unanswered at the time of writing, was whether or not there was a Red Cross or other identifier on the roof of Darwin Hospital. According to Harry Dale, Kates over Town released their bombs simultaneously. Since the Barracks at Larrakeyah were at the far end of the attack zone, Dale had fingered the leading Kates as the offenders. Kate attacks were always led by Fuschida and Fuschida had promised the Emperor that, as a matter of Japanese Honour, hospitals would not be bombed. The reader is left to play jury but in the mind of the author Japan has the benefit of the doubt.

To his credit, Lou Curnock kept coastal radio station VID broadcasting from Frog's Hollow during the blitz. At 10:05am the Deputy Postal Director in Darwin, Mr Fanning, used VID to radio Senator Ashley, the Post Master General, saying, "The Town is being raided and the broadcasting station is closing down." His message was passed on quickly to Lieutenant General Sturdee, Chief of the General Staff.

Citizens knew the town was defenceless with an air raid protection system aborted by its civil administration. With such psychologically unprepared occupants panic was inevitable.

The Kate Raid left 35 dead in Town and numerous casualties.

When it appeared that the bombing on Town had stopped, Judge Alexander Wells drove to Fannie Bay Gaol and ordered the release of prisoners. Prisoner Ivan Sinclair, who had previously been a hospital orderly and wound-dresser, was put on temporary release attached to police rescue operations. He worked straight through for five days administering first aid and retrieving bodies from the mangrove swamps before crocodile or shark got them. Prime Minister John Curtin later signed the authority giving Sinclair a full pardon. His crime was Murder.

When the Blitz began, Ludo Dalby was driving the *Dunny Truck*. He and the doffers shared a shelter with others who had no choice in the matter. It might have been something one of the others said about Japanese troops landing as soon as the bombing finished. Ludo and the doffers felt grateful that their families had been evacuated. As soon as the bombers passed, Ludo and the doffers bolted to the half-full truck and raced for Adelaide River, 75 miles south. Thus, the Darwin Dunny Truck started the Adelaide River Stakes, and others joined the race filling the road with every kind of vehicle and some on foot. Just south of town a road grader joined in and was running second to Ludo. Ludo, determined to come first, took a bend too fast and the Dunny Truck rolled throwing Ludo, doffers and produce into a stock take. The Darwin Dunny Truck won line honours in the Adelaide River Stakes.

CHAPTER 11
AIRFIELD RAID

10.08am to 10.25am

There were 2000 Allied Personnel at RAAF Base and Civil Aerodrome. Most aircraft were not camouflaged. The aim for the second wave of 27 Kate Bombers was to kill as many as possible while destroying assets. The Kates arrived from the southeast to find 19 aircraft parked at the RAAF and Civil aerodromes. They pattern bombed RAAF Base and were gone within minutes. When the first bomb hit No.13 Squadron hangar, leaving a Wirraway with severe shrapnel damage, the RAAF Station Commander Sturt Griffith looked at the time. It was 10.08am. At RAAF Base the high level bombing caused extensive surface damage levelling the recreation hall and surrounding buildings, hangars and air traffic control facilities. Other damage is difficult to allocate between this high level raid and the one which followed. For this reason it has been reported with the last high level raid.

During this attack Bruce Ackland and Ted Betts ran to the DCA radio room and, while bombs were falling on the airport, sent out an encoded message via the DCA Aeradio station at Cloncurry:

"DARWIN BOMBED MACHINE GUNNED 20 JAPS 30XMNS 1000 NINETEEN CIVIL BUILDINGS AND RADIO ROOM MINOR DAMAGE FIRE TENDER HANGAR SOME RAAF BS7GS BURNT DROME OK THINK ELEVEN MILE OK ALL STAFF OK STOP" BETTS.

While Kates were Bombing RAAF Base, 17 Val Bombers and 9 Zeros on their way to the civil aerodrome diverted to attack the infrastructure hub at Berrimah. Bombs knocked out the overland telegraph station and disrupted the Naval Communications Headquarters at Coonawarra.

The Army Field Hospital at Berrimah was located directly in line with Runway 11-29 at the airport, about a mile from the runway threshold. There were four light machine gun emplacements surrounding the hospital, an invitation for disaster. Zeros were strafing these gun posts when stray fire inevitably raked four hospital wards, one patient dying soon after. If the pilots were deliberately targeting the hospital, casualties would have been far greater than this.

At one of these posts gunner Wilbert (Darky) Hudson, with a guiding hand from his mates, brought down a Zero with his Lewis Gun resting on an empty 44-gallon drum out in the open, the Zero crashing near *Coonawarra*. This being the first enemy aircraft destroyed over Australian soil, Hudson was awarded the Military Medal.

Nearby, the 54th Searchlight Battery had a searchlight at Lake Ironstone, defended by Lance Corporal F. Terone assisted by Sapper Dick Spedding. Their only weapon was a Lewis Machine Gun with a small supply of ammunition. Between them they managed to get a deadly aim on an incoming Zero and shot it down. Fuschida said that he lost seven aircraft during the Battle. Allied accounting lists six. The seventh was the Terone-Spedding kill.

Zeros were concentrating on military field emplacements, machine guns and searchlights. At Winellie just south of the airfield 4 zeros were locked in a dual with 4 Hotchkiss light machine gun posts. Zeros were flying so low over gun emplacements that gunners and pilots were often looking eye to eye. This developed into a cavalier attitude on both sides, exchanging forked-fingers-of-fury as a passing gesture. Trooper Max Grant tracked a Zero, gunner Allan Weidner watching for the pilot's gesture, gestured back yelling 'fire it up his arse!' and Grant shot it down.

With Kate raids over, Zeros returned to strafe everything. One Zero was cutting up slit trenches out by the runway when the popular Wing Commander Archie Tindal sprang from a trench with a light machine gun to shoot it down from the hip. Tindal was blown to shreds by a single cannon shell. He was the first Australian RAAF officer killed in battle on Australian soil.

Vals dived on the Civil and Military aerodromes scoring a direct hit on the hangar of No 12 Squadron, wrecking 3 US C-45 transports one after the other and a US LB-30 bomber with a direct hit. A sequence of Vals dived in a frenzy of destruction and kept bombing until all their targets were destroyed and burning: six Lockheed Hudsons, three Beechcrafts. The Kate attack over Town knocked out Pylons and transmission lines near the mains power plant at Stuart Park, leaving radio sets at RAAF Base and Civil aerodrome on their emergency backup generators, but radios were jammed.

Zeros destroyed three Wirraway fighters undergoing maintenance at the Civil Aerodrome. Buildings, hangars and equipment went up in smoke. A privately owned de Havilland Puss Moth VH-UPN was destroyed. One Zero overran the air field and strafed the small medical centre hospital at Bagot. Vals were using a cocktail of anti-personnel daisy-cutter, high-explosion and incendiary bombs. The Oil Store was soon on fire, a freshening wind blowing the flames towards the Administration Building setting it on fire. Ackland, Betts and Tarlton sprung from their trench and started for the radio room to rescue the DCA radio transmitters and receivers but were forced back when a bomb hit the ammunition dump and bullets started firing every which-way. As the arsenal firing faded, the three DCA officers, still exposed to attacking aircraft and a burning building salvaged the radio equipment; but the bombing had knocked out the DCA emergency power supply and mains power was already cut. Eventually they cleverly restored communications by setting up a link to Aeradio VID and sent a coded message to Melbourne via the civil aerodrome in Daly Waters. They worked around the clock to restore communications in the Darwin area.

Zeros unleashed vengeful machine gun attacks knocking out more than half the searchlights supporting the antiaircraft positions around the Town and aerodromes. This was an indicator that the Japanese were planning night attacks which, unless it were a foil, suggested that troop landings were unlikely.

At RAAF Base water and emergency electric power survived these attacks.

CHAPTER 12
SECOND RAID ON HARBOUR

First of Three Val Bomber Attacks
10.08am to 10.18am

The first run began for 27 olive green dive bombers, escorted by 9 Zeros, whose mission was to attack all vessels, seaplanes and infrastructure along the harbour. The prize target was *Houston* undergoing repairs to her rear turret. This would be a golden opportunity to sink *Houston*. As ever, she would be fast off the mark with deadly fire power but, in port, she would not have room for the brilliant evasive tactics she showed at sea. Japanese intelligence had not yet found her hiding place so every pilot was on the lookout for her.

Two Patwing 10 Catalinas left behind by *William B. Preston* were still at anchor, their crews preparing as fast as possible for takeoff. Incoming Zeros sunk them, killing one crewman and leaving the rest to scramble into life-rafts. The Zeros did not return to strafe the life-rafts.

Vals were working in pairs, attacking a ship from two ends or two sides to divide and frustrate its fire power.

Warrego had raised steam, knocked the pins out of the cable holding her anchor and, leaving her anchor on the bed of the harbour began evasive tactics putting up a sheet of gun fire that Vals preferred to avoid.

On *Karangi* gunner Harry Dale watched as Zero machine gun fire raked through the water starboard. Vals and Zeros were soon driven away by the proximity and intensity of anti aircraft fire from *Karangi*. One of Dale's shots made the tail of a Val wobble but no kill.

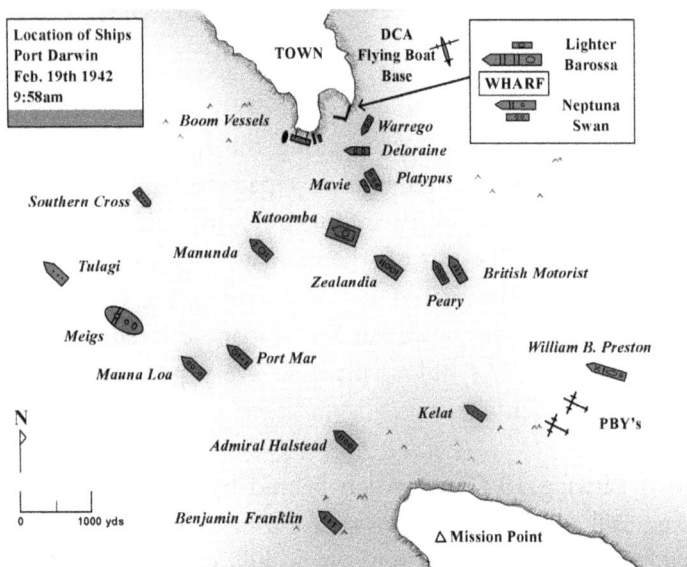

Location of Ships

Swan under Lieutenant Commander Alan J. Travis had been transferring antiaircraft shells directly from *Neptuna* but pulled away quickly when the Kate bombing started. With Vals descending on her, *Swan* was shooting her way out of the inner port supported by sheets of anti aircraft fire from the 2/14th AA Battery on the oval. The 14th found that their guns were too slow for targets in their ninety degree arc across the harbour. The shell fuses set at the minimum 2 seconds were exploding too late. The range needed was much less than this. Jack Mulholland changed the fuse time to a risky 1.5 seconds just as *Swan* was under attack from a Val. The Val was caught in a cone of fire with the new fuse time exploding near its nose. The Val was seen side slipping northeast across the harbour to crash in the sea north of East Point. The 14th cheered. The crew on *Swan* cheered. Swan moved on and was soon in the company of her sister ship *Warrego*. The dive bombers descended upon them and they fought back valiantly. Swan avoided direct hits but three near misses killed three men and injured 19. She was damaged but would live to fight another day. *Warrego* was low on ammunition but made it through unscathed.

On this first bombing run Vals and Zeros approaching along East Arm bypassed the Norwegian Tanker *Benjamin Franklin*. An accompanying factor was her location on the other side of Mission Point behind Peak Hill but they also bypassed *Kelat* in view off the end of Mission Point. The focus seemed to be on *Admiral Hulstead*, raising steam but still moored between *Benjamin Franklin* and *Kelat*. A factor was *Admiral Hulstead's* cargo which made her a key target on the first bombing run. As told earlier:

Two Val dive bombers, working as a pair, attacked Admiral Halstead from the stern on two sides. Johnson was determined to spare his cargo of 14,000 drums of aviation gasoline and petrol for Army vehicles but the dual attack would halve the intensity of his machine gun fire. He was about to split his fire when his luck changed. McMahon's Kittyhawk did a half roll pointing its nose at one Val and began shooting tracer at it, leaving Johnson, who could see the tracer, at full fire power on the other Val. After McMahon attacked, he saw the rear gunner in the Val slump over his gun. A Zero attacked McMahon's Kittyhawk forcing him to take cover in nearby cloud.

British Motorist and Peary. Sky shows attacking Vals,
AA blast and white dots are flack from HMAS Karangi
From the Collection of Petty Officer H.E.S. 'Nobby' Clark by
courtesy of Major Faye Clark WRAAC (ret.) OAM RFD.

British Motorist was refuelling *Peary* but terminated the refuelling operation after Kates attacked the inner port. At this time *British Motorist* and *Peary* were side by side facing the inner harbour. In a surprise attack, a pair of Vals swooped on them from behind. Two direct hits forward on *British Motorist* killed her Master Gilbert Bates, radio operator James Webster and wounded many of the remaining 59 British seamen. To evade further bombing she swung away from *Peary*, her propellers fluttering furiously as she backed into the harbour. *British Motorist* was leaking oil from her port side and caught fire. Near misses bomb splashed *Peary*. She manoeuvred away and opened anti-aircraft fire driving off Vals that were swooping one after another, again and again.

Neptuna had berthed on the outer limb at Stokes Hill wharf before 9am and wharfies had just started to discharge her cargo. In the panic hatch Nos. 1, 3 and 4 had been left open. The stowage was 200 ton of depth charges, two ton of TNT, magazines of anti aircraft ammunition and timber. *Neptuna* had taken superficial secondary damage from the Kate attack. A pair of Vals suddenly appeared from behind a cloud bank. *Neptuna* lookouts were caught by surprise as a Val attack was suddenly in progress. The first Val dived at her stern aligning with the length of the ship and dropped a 250kg bomb which sliced through her bridge into the saloon killing 45 including her Master William Mitchie who was lying mortally wounded on the upper deck. Below deck, falling debris left Dr John Hyde and Cadet John Rothery with their legs pinned. In the engine room, engineers and stokers were amongst the wounded, some seriously. They were powering up the starboard engine but had to abandon this work leaving *Neptuna* immobile. Third Officer Deburca had taken command. Deburca had the Chinese crew members assembling a makeshift gangway onto the wharf using hatch planking.

The second Val attacking *Neptuna* dropped its 250kg bomb straight through Hatch No 1 which had been left open. It fell into a cargo of timber starting a fire which spread quickly as stokers and other crew scurried for the upper deck. It also sent a shudder shaking the ship and redistributing existing damage so that Hyde and Rothery were freed. They found their way up to the main deck where the fire on board was spreading and Deburca had dropped the gangway idea, called "abandon ship" and was handing out life vests for survivors to exit over the side.

Neptuna started to list throwing Hyde and Rothery overboard clinging to hatch planks in the water. Hyde was alarmed as patches of burning oil started to edge up to his face and he thought he was a goner. His experience was shared by another 80 seamen from *Neptuna.*

Like a reflex requiring no thought, Coxswain John Waldie was on the spot in DCA launch C22. While his boatman steadied the launch Waldie, with endless energy, was dragging survivors aboard. As he looked at their faces black with oil and their oil-damaged eyes, he said later that he "couldn't tell if they were Japanese, Chinese or Filipino." He sensed their lives struggling for life itself and worked faster and faster to get them aboard. His shuttle became unstable with more than 30 passengers and his boatman was doing a good job ducking the fires. After Waldie dragged Hyde and Rothery aboard, the shuttle was full. He made directly for the beach and unloaded quickly. As servicemen were arriving to help, Dr John Hyde, ignoring his own injury, began treatment of the injured and was awarded an OBE and Lloyds War Medal for heroism in treating the injured at the battle of Darwin. Rothery fell onto pebbles and passed away. Waldie spun C22 towards *Neptuna* to continue the rescue.

During the Kate attack a near miss damaged Naval Headquarters on the foreshore but the Signal Station was not damaged. As Lieutenant Commander Ethridge Grant was leaving the building with no way of reaching *William B. Preston*, he was met by Lieutenant Ian McRoberts who was driving the DCA passenger shuttle C2. McRoberts was looking for volunteers to help him with rescue operations. He already had two volunteers and Ethridge Grant became the third. McRoberts spun C2 back into the inner harbour to help Waldie, starting with survivors holding on to structural sections under the wharf. The ebbing tide had been clearing fires away from the wharf making a safer access for rescue work there.

The fire on *Neptuna* was intense and spread to MV *Barossa* moored opposite *Neptuna* on the inner limb of Stokes Hill Wharf. The situation was complex, and anti-aircraft fire from the Oval, *Warrego, Deloraine* and *Platypus* covered Tug *Wato,* under the command of Warrant Officer Andrew Gibson, while she untangled the mess.

It became complex like this: Before the Kate attack, a Lighter came alongside Barossa to take on oil from a pipeline that ran from the Oil Farm out along the wharf. As Kates bombed the Wharf, HMAS *Kiara* was handy and started rescue operations from the inner side. Just before Vals commenced hostilities *Kiara's* engine broke down leaving her to the whims of the ebbing tide and a danger to all in her path. She dropped anchor pulling her up alongside the Lighter. This was how the inner limb of the wharf became three ships deep while the outer limb was two ships deep until Swan cleared away from *Neptuna*. During the first Val attack on the harbour *Wato* towed *Kiara* into the outer port while the Oil Tank Farm blazed on one side, *Neptuna* came under attack on the other side, chunks of wharf debris threatened her propellers, civilian motor-boats crisscrossed in front of her and enemy planes were looking for an opportunity with her. *Wato* left *Kiara*, towed the Lighter away and started to help *Barossa* from her mooring while the crew abandoned ship by lifeboat.

Kiara was soon in trouble ebbing in burning oil, her prospects fading fast, until she was rescued by a Stores Lighter, the lugger HMAS *Yampi Lass*. *Yampi Lass* was hosting deep sea diver J.E. Johnstone, a renowned treasure hunter. *Yampi Lass* towed *Kiara* to safety.

Nearby, *Platypus,* which had the most strident klaxon in the fleet, continued a deep-throated, mournful, *'whoop whoop'* warning of the Val attack. As if in reprisal, a Val attacked her by the stern and she took a full stick of three bombs. The near miss 30 ft off port sank RAN patrol lugger Mavie, which was tied to her amidships, and a flight of fragments from *Mavie* shattered the quarter deck awnings on *Platypus* killing 2 sailors. A near miss aft went under the *Platypus* stern. The normally happy crew on *Platypus* had not panicked but those who saw this bomb were genuflecting or murmuring prayers as they waited for unconsciousness, wondering if they would even hear the explosion. The bomb did not explode. The near miss starboard damaged her condensers so badly that she lost all steam. On the ebbing tide the only evasive strategy remaining for Platypus was to keep swinging around her anchor buoy. J P Tonkin, Commander of *Platypus,* watched Petty Officer Bartlett and the three ratings from *Mavie* swim to the floating deck. Tonkin sent a work party to bring them below to the Tender's hospital where legendary surgeon Dr Darcy Sutherland would treat their injuries.

McRoberts and Grant in C2 landed their first 30 survivors on the beach.

Zealandia lifeboats, manned by ship's volunteers, were on

rescue work picking up survivors being swept away with the burning tide. Val pilots trying to attack *Zealandia* had to postpone their bombs. Their caution was astute because *Zealandia* was surrounded by ships with deadly anti-aircraft fire: William B. Preston on the south, *Katoomba* in the Floating Dry Dock to the west, *Swan*, *Platypus* and *Karangi* to the north and to the east there was *Peary* with *British Motorist* blocking the attack path.

Camouflaged fuel storage tanks were imbedded in the low cliffs around the edge of the inner harbour. The 19th Machine Gun Regiment were deployed to defend the beach and tanks. *Katoomba* was sitting in the floating dry dock off shore from these fuel tanks flanked by the Lewis machine guns of the 19th.

Katoomba and *Deloraine* had destroyed IJN submarine I-124 a few weeks earlier. The Captain of *Deloraine* Lieutenant Commander D.A. Menlove was awarded a DSO. While pursuing a second submarine *Katoomba* collided with US tanker *Pecos* and was now in floating dry dock awaiting repairs. She was a stationary target but this also steadied the aim of her anti- aircraft fire.

A pair of Vals took her on, attacked from two sides, the starboard attack coming first. Her cunning Captain Cousins already had a 12 pounder shell primed on a short fuse and timed one shot to perfection. The pilot saw it coming, dropped his bomb prematurely and swerved out of harm's way. By the time the other Val attacked Cousins had the port machine guns backed up with auxiliary gun fire and again the Val released early to veer out of harm's way. *Katoomba* took some damage but no direct hits. Cousins knew how important it was to defend the Floating Dry Dock from damage.

Cousins was keeping an eye on other vessels, following the course of battle and its significance for his ship. He knew about *Neptuna's* dangerous cargo, saw the fire spreading on her decks and ordered his crew to take cover against likely shrapnel from *Neptuna*. His wisdom would soon be proved.

Along the outer moorings merchant transport vessels from the *Houston* convoy were in a long straight queue waiting to unload. They were vulnerable. These ships were armed merchantmen and their crews were ready to fight for the troops, seamen and extensive military cargo they were carrying.

First in line was *Port Mar*. Her crew were late manning her four 5" mounts, four 40mm and 16 20mm AA guns. She took a hit killing a seaman and wounding others. Hull plates ruptured at the water line. To avoid sinking in deep water with all her equipment on board, *Port Mar* steered towards the beach, sinking slowly, which allowed troops to abandon ship. *Zeros* swept on her strafing her decks, wounding several seamen and leaving all her lifeboats shredded.

Second in line was *Mauna Loa*. She had been damaged in the Houston convoy two days earlier when near misses riddled the port lifeboats, holed her hull and sent fragment strikes as high as the wheel house. Her guns were firing continuously but Vals, attacking out of the Sun, put two bombs down No.5 hatch breaking her back. In one action Zeros and Vals strafed her decks killing 5 of her 38 crew. She was holed and sinking.

Third in line was *Meigs,* the largest vessel in harbour (13,000t). She was attacked by two pair of Vals coming from four sides and was hit directly again and again, killing 2 of her 66 crew. She caught fire but had been badly holed. Her huge steel hull ruptured; the cargo of munitions, railway lines, Bren gun carriers and trucks became dangerously dislodged. She sank within minutes. Her crew abandoned ship leaving her to sink slowly in a warm blue shroud of tropical sea water, the cargo of military hardware with her.

Metal fragments from these blasts, together with a near miss minutes later, damaged *Tulagi* killing three US soldiers from the 148th Artillery Regiment of the Idaho National Guard: James Wofferd, Wilbur Meade and Robert Steeton. Vals and Zeros attacking Tulagi faced light fire from ship's machine guns but as they approached, the Idaho gunners on deck, ignoring their exposure to strafing, opened multiple heavy machine gun fire. This surprise tactic drove off Zeros and caused early bomb releases from Vals. Australian Merchantman Tulagi was spared thanks to the bravery of the Idaho 148th Field Artillery Regiment.

It was *William B. Preston's* turn. The flying boat tender had upped anchor and proceeded towards the boom gate passing south of *British motorist* alongside *Peary*. She was on the run to the open sea, fast off the mark, *zigzagging* through a crowded harbour. Her lookouts spotted the formations of Vals. The crew took down the awnings which shielded them from the sun. This uncovered her four water cooled Browning machine guns. She opened fire which seemed to discourage some of the attackers but others continued relentlessly. Four bombs exploded off her bow shattering the windows on her bridge killing eleven, one sailor severed in half at the waist. Two were missing. A well aimed bomb hit aft just forward of the after deckhouse wounding three, two fatally. There were secondary explosions. Her fire power was all but destroyed. She lost steering control forward and had to rely on Lester Wood's skill in coordinating the port and starboard engines, marginally assisted by directly steering a jammed rudder. At 10.15am a radio message came through from her Patwing 22 Catalina patrolling north along the boundary between the Timor and Arafura Seas. It reported a fleet of four Japanese carriers, screened by battleships and cruisers, latitude 10.25degS and longitude 129.21degE.

About 300 yards from the crippled *William B. Preston*, *Peary* had slipped anchor, raised steam and was on the move. She had spent the night hunting a submarine and her crew was frustrated by lack of success. They were tired and slow to react until bomb splashes renewed their sense of survival. Morale was as low as their expletive language. They hated 'Japs': had killed many. 'Japs' now trying to bomb them were more than aggravating. Sailors manned battle stations and all guns opened fire on any Val or Zero within range. The feeling was mutual. To the Japanese *Peary* was 'public enemy number two' after *Houston* and they were looking for *Houston* hoping that *Peary* would lead them to her. Four Vals were on standby to attack *Houston* and P*eary's* reluctance to join her suggested that *Houston* was still hiding. Perhaps *Houston* would come out of hiding to spare *Peary*. Japanese accuracy marked *Peary* for destruction. The bombers dived and wheeled, dived and wheeled, unleashing their bombs one at a time on *Peary* until every bomb was dropped. The screening Zeros raided and raided with cannon and tracer. The first two bombs were direct hits tearing off her propeller guards, dislodging her depth-charge racks, flooding her steering motor room and delivering an incendiary explosion in her galley deckhouse. The third bomb was a fizzer but sliced through her deck and holed her hull. A high-explosive bomb forward was a direct hit sending her magazines skyward in a rage of high explosion. The fifth bomb was an incendiary setting her engine room ablaze. Plumes of dense black smoke belched continuously from her stern but as some sailors abandoned ship others kept her guns firing, particularly the forward ack-ack. Peary had lost all power and steering, the ebbing tide carrying her out along the channel towards the ship nearest to her: hospital ship *Manunda*.

Harry Dale on *Karangi* near *Peary* later wrote to his mother that *"Peary* took a direct hit on her magazines and was blown sky high. I've got bells in my ears." *Karangi* was closed up at action stations giving all her fire power to help Peary. About forty of *Peary's* crew jumped overboard, a *Zealandia* lifeboat and Examination Steamer *Southern Cross* coming to the rescue.

Coxswain John Waldie on C22 now had a full shuttle, mainly Chinese seamen from *Neptuna*. It had taken some time for Waldie and his boatman to drag them from the sea because he had to zigzag several times to avoid Zero strafing and then come back to the victims who were ebbing with the tide. He saved most of the 62 Chinese seamen that day. Waldie saw the *Barossa* lifeboat passing the end of the Wharf carrying their injured. He quickly realised that the lifeboat was not motorized and was being carried away by the ebbing fire-tide faster than its crew could row. If that continued the lifeboat would end up in flames. Waldie pointed this out to his boatman who quickly announced that there was no more room on the shuttle, the rescued uninjured quickly concurring. Waldie spun C22 up to the bow of the Barossa lifeboat and threw them a line. At that moment Neptuna started rumbling. To the Chinese it sounded like a hungry dragon. Waldie opened the throttle heading for the beach with a full shuttle and lifeboat in tow. He kept a lookout for strafing Zeros but the attack seemed to be over.

Brisbane Man Saved 150 Lives

CANBERRA, Friday.—For bravery during air raids on Darwin in 1942, Mr. John F. Waldie, 25, of Cleveland Street, Coorparoo, Brisbane, and of the Civil Aviation Department, has been awarded the British Empire Medal (civil division).

As coxswain, Waldie, accompanied by a boathand, manned a civil aviation launch and brought ashore ship crews and wharf labourers from vessels which had been bombed. He then carried on alone for three trips, rescuing about 30 people each trip besides towing lifeboats full of men. Later he made further rescues and was instrumental in saving 150 lives in all.

Coxswain John Waldie

By the time the first dive bomber raid was over the fire on *Neptuna* had spread aft and into the hold at hatch No.3. The 200 ton of depth charges and two ton of TNT went up in a seething rage of explosion. All at once bellows of dense black smoke, shot full of flames, mushroomed 700 feet upwards, mushroomed with a tight symmetric bloom atop a thick and upward stem still furiously full of flames, a mushroom that was going to be fed further by the secondary explosions of magazines. A side-plate took off like a missile and landed 300 yards away on the foreshore. White hot railings shot across the harbour imbedding in *Katoomba*. *Neptuna's* ripped out mast and lifeboats, swirling around amongst other debris in the bellows of smoke, were tossed on high trajectories to targets unknown. A shock wave concussed *Deloraine* and *Platypus*. *Platypus* escaped serious debris damage but *Deloraine,* at the mooring closest to *Neptuna* was struck by metal fragments. The sound intensity of the explosion was more than deafening. Its victims felt brain belted as if they were the epicentre of all noise in the universe. The blast was heard across Darwin's bays, Darwin's town and airport, and masked the agonizing screams that came with punctured ears. Survivors still in the sound-magnifying sea, who were already blinded, distressed and disoriented, struggling to chose between death by drowning and death from facial burning, were delivered such a violent impact that many were rendered unconscious, delivered to the flames if they had a life vest, the depths if not and some were mercifully killed outright.

Neptuna was ripped in half. Her stern and engines sank beside the wharf; her bow floated briefly then turned on its side and sank.

Neptuna Explodes - From the Collection of Petty Officer H.E.S. 'Nobby' Clark by courtesy of Major Faye Clark WRAAC (ret.) OAM RFD.

The explosion also destroyed a long section of the inner limb of the wharf where *Barossa* was at last being towed clear by tug *Wato*. *Barossa* started to take water through buckled steel plates dislodged from her hull. *Wato* towed *Barossa* away from what was left of the wharf. *Wato* was struggling but the brave Auxiliary Minesweeper HMAS *Tolga* relieved *Wato*, took *Barossa* under tow and beached her.

CHAPTER 13

ROAD-KILL ON THE AERIAL-HIGHWAY

The second dive bomber raid across the harbour was coming as 27 Vals, fresh and fully armed, arrived in the next wave from the southeast.

Vals from the first raid weren't done yet but they had to clear the decks to give the incoming squadrons room to move. They took a ten minute flight path circling around to come in again from the southeast for a third raid across the harbour. They still had bombs to drop: Two Vals were holding their bombs for *Zealandia;* four were still primed and ready to go as soon as they found *Houston*, and many had 60kg bombs to deliver. Zeros remained over the harbour to support the second raid, some straying to attack land based targets, all trying to spot *Houston*.

As the circling Vals flew past Fannie Bay they were exposed to cones of ground fire from a 2/14th Heavy Ant-Aircraft post but made it through unharmed. They were half way round when a Kittyhawk, six wing cannons blazing, attacked out of the Sun and shot down a Val. The Zeros were busy machine gunning search lights and the Kitty Hawk had time to attack another Val, maybe a kill, but the Zeros had woken up. The Kitty Hawk retreated hurriedly into the Sun to hover, as hawks do, waiting for another kill on the aerial highway.

Lieutenant Robert Oestreicher knew that the range of his fuel tanks exceeded those of the Zeros and they would leave before he had to land. He believed that the two Vals, travelling south when he shot them down, were heading for the airfield at Batchelor where the RAAF had stationed nine fully functional Wirraway fighters.

CHAPTER 14
THIRD RAID ON HARBOUR

Second of Three Attacks by Vals
10:18am to 10:32am

At this stage of the battle, 22 Allied ships were damaged, sunk or sinking and there was more to come.

When 27 fresh Vals entered the harbour along East Arm at 10:18am they were greeted by 3/8ths cloud cover below 2,000ft and poor visibility. Debris fines and dust were scattering the light. Smoke from burning oil and burning ships was reducing visibility over the water.

British Motorist rolled over, sank at her mooring, and no longer blocked access to *Zealandia*.

Zealandia's hatches were open and ammunition from No.1 hatch was left on deck to expedite unloading. A pair of Vals attacked her stern, one each side. Bombs fell through hatch No 4, the engine room skylight and an incendiary set her lower deck on fire near No.3 hatch storing anti-tank weapons yet to be unloaded. Three of her 142 seamen were killed. The fire started to spread. In response the fire crew aimed their hoses to stop the fire reaching forward to hatch No.1 storing anti-tank ammunition. The next bomb hit the steam lines that drove the pumps for the fire hoses. The final group to be evacuated included Patrick Vincent O'Connor, 27, fireman and able bodied seaman James Masson, 61, both of the Australian Merchant Navy. These seamen were badly burnt and wounded.

Before Kerr had them transferred to his last lifeboat running a ferry service to *Manunda*, he called the remaining seamen to help him wave down rescuers to abandon ship.

Platypus still looked dangerous with her heavy machine guns at the ready. As a pair of Vals approached, *Wato,* which had completed her mission with *Barossa*, was passing close to *Platypus.* The Vals released two 250kg bombs on *Platypus* with *Wato* as second prize. The bombs arrived simultaneously, one each side of *Wato* sending up a thirty-foot fountain wave. On top of the wave was *Wato.* Fountain descended leaving Wato airborne but catching up. *Wato* made a soft landing and steamed on as if nothing had happened. Lookouts on *Platypus* clapped. This was their second miracle that day.

On *Manunda* the wounded started to arrive, 76 that day and 190 the next. Dentist Captain Hocking and Nursing Officer Margaret De Mestre might typically be helping three surgeons to triage on the reception deck. These medical soldiers were professionals with extensive experience from the *Manunda's* service to British and other allied soldiers during campaigns in the Middle East, Mediterranean and Africa. First priority was given to casualties where immediate medical treatment was a matter of life or death, or soon would be. Many injuries were oil blindness and burns and all patients were suffering shock. These injuries complicated assessment of other injuries especially where haemorrhaging wounds or amputations required intravenous access to administer transfusion or other liquid resuscitation. These cases were quickly prepared, triaged for one of the five operating theatres, and delivered promptly.

Nurses on the arrival deck, assisted by orderlies, were working first aid points for the walking wounded. After treatment, these patients were invited to sit aside on the reception deck, deck zero.

Those beyond help, many with burns to more than 50% of the surface area of their body were made comfortable on a cocktail of morphine, a sympathetic young nurse, a cigarette and Chaplain John Blakemore. The harbour was littered with dead bodies and body parts, some washing up on the beach but most carried away on a 3kn ebbing fire-tide with its stench of burning flesh.

Consider, if you will, a painting of *Manunda*. She had a stubby yellow funnel with a small red cross each side barely higher than the lifeboats. There were red crosses on her deck. Her hull was white with a decorative dark olive band around the top. Small red crosses on white circles, three each side, were evenly spaced along the hull but the red crosses were not only centred in the middle of the dark band, the size of these crosses was barely greater than the band width. Hold this picture for a moment while we paint some background.

Blazing fuel oil racing from the Oil Tank Farm became a 3kn fire-tide following the main channel towards the Boom-net. As the fire-tide drew its veil of smoke northwest around *Manunda* her red crosses were still visible from the north but difficult to make out from the south. *Peary* ebbed past *Manunda*. *Peary* was belching large volumes of dense smoke from her stern which dramatically thickened the oil smoke already around her. Volumes of combined smoke carried on the northwest breeze screening *Manunda*, particularly from the south. *Peary's* decks were a-wash but her forward ack-

ack gunner was still firing. When he saw *Manunda* being screened it reminded him that *Peary* often made smoke for *Houston*. The tactic usually drew Japanese aircraft closer trying to identify a target in the smoke, hopefully a merchant vessel with vital cargo, a troop carrier or crippled cruiser. When, like a ghost, *Houston* sprang from the smoke, her guns scored heavily against such short range targets. Japanese aircraft had been snared by this tactic.

Let's paint the sky.

USS Peary rounding HMAHS Manunda - From the Collection of Petty Officer H.E.S. 'Nobby' Clark by courtesy of Major Faye Clark WRAAC (ret.) OAM RFD.

High in the sky, the Japanese had been struggling to find Houston. During earlier bombing runs, as pilots searched for Houston, they all saw the markings on *Manunda*, left her alone but knew where she was permanently anchored. Their Spy in Darwin had confirmed the findings of yesterday's reconnaissance aircraft. *Houston* returned with her convoy to Port Darwin and was under repair, but where? This morning's Japanese reconnaissance had failed due to radio problems and the reconnaissance aircraft was still flying back to Ceram with today's update.

Although this was the third bombing run over the harbour, it was the first for these Val pilots and they were holding altitude in the south and east ready for bombing runs away from heavy anti-aircraft fire on the northern side of the harbour. At this stage there was a lot of smoke and *Houston* knew how to hide in smoke. What was *Peary* screening? Was it the old trick with *Houston?* They radioed pilots from the previous bombing runs and were told that the hospital ship was nearly a mile west of *Peary.* Anyway, *Peary* wouldn't deliberately put smoke over a hospital ship. Her crew would have seen that this was the third Harbour attack and the hospital ship had been spared every time.

On *Manunda* triaging continued below deck away from the smoke. It is easy to imagine the dentist Captain Hocking assisted by RAAN Officer Margaret De Mestre working on Gunner James Dee from the 2/14th Field Regiment.

Captain Cousins, watching from the Dry Dock north of *Manunda*, saw a Val coming at him from the south in a direct line over *Manunda* but suddenly realised that Vals were deliberately attacking *Manunda*. This Val was one of a pair. The first bomb was a near miss. Four people were killed from shrapnel across the decks and her plates were perforated with 76 holes.

The first Val passed north of *Manunda* to ascend and circle back to the south. As it did so, the rear gunner could make out red crosses on *Manunda*. In a panic he called off the second Val whose crew believed they were attacking *Houston*. It was all too late. The second bomb just missed the bridge and exploded on B and C decks destroying the medical and nursing staff quarters, hitting one of the aid posts, damaging the navigational equipment and disabling her lifts. Bomb splinters cut all her fire mains; glass was shattered all over the deck. Fires broke out causing terrible burn wounds and the crew lowered life boats to rescue casualties who had been flung into the water. Hocking, De Mestre and Dee were killed and the physiotherapist, Joan McKillop suffered a compound fracture to one of her legs. The aggregate toll on *Manunda* personnel was now eleven killed and 58 wounded: one mortally and 18 seriously. Manunda continued to function as a hospital. She was left alone for the rest of this raid and on the following raid.

Japanese pilots were more than embarrassed; Fuschida was going to have their guts for garters. They blamed *Houston* which was somewhere in port but hiding and they blamed *Peary* which fled the crime scene on the tide, her decks awash, her .30in and .50in machine guns fighting back from the galley deckhouse, her forward ack-ack exchanging machine gun fire at will. *Peary's* forward ack-ack paused briefly while an officer replaced the fallen gunner. Her forward ack-ack resumed. Fifteen minutes later, as her stern slipped beneath the sea, her bow rose, her forward ack-ack firing until water lapped the base of the gun. The officer on the gun was dragged under briefly by the sinking *Peary* soon to reappear floating alive in his life vest. Her losses were 4 officers and 76 enlisted sailors killed or drowned with 52 survivors many of whom were injured, eleven fatally.

Admiral Halstead was used to looking after herself. Her cargo of 14,000 drums of high octane aviation gasoline had to be spared. Her Master Teddy Johnson led a team of six that could keep machine guns firing with skill. Three near misses caused her light damage, more significantly, no fire. If the Japanese realised the volatility of her cargo their lack of luck with this ship must have been agonising.

The Australian corvettes and sloops: *Vigilant, Warnambool, Tolga, Terka* and *Southern Cross* and the spare Boom vessels had spread out on rescue operations. Three Vals dived on *Southern Cross* as she was rescuing survivors from *Peary.* They released their seven bombs one at a time and strafed her. From the viewpoint of the zigzagging *Southern Cross* she was attacked seven times taking significant damage for a 298t ship but still floating. Seamen Breen, Purdon and Sault were fatally burnt. Her Captain, Lieutenant Commander C.F. Symonds was mentioned in despatches for his courage leading a brave and devoted crew to pick up *Peary* survivors.

On *Mauna Loa* operational lifeboats had been scarce since many were strafed by Japanese aircraft during the Houston convoy. Captain F. R. Trask got a starboard life boat and a work boat away with all hands.

Port Mar and the Burns Phillip motor vessel *Tulagi* beached near Channel Island Leprosarium.

The crippled Catalina Tender *William B. Preston* eventually made it to the Boom-net gate where *Gunbar* had left to help *Port Mar* but *Kangaroo* was standing to. As *William B. Preston* passed through the gate *Kangaroo* covered her escape with all the anti-aircraft fire she had. In return, a Zero strafed *Kangaroo* killing one of her sailors. *William B. Preston* turned west and made for the open sea, her cargo of bombs and gasoline in tact.

On *Manunda* Matron Clara Shumack, who had been outstanding in her management of the hospital under pressure came up to deck zero coughing in thick smoke from fires aboard. Shumack saw bodies everywhere and was visibly upset by the loss of her friend Margaret de Mestre. Clara went to her knees and wept. Suddenly she stood to her feet and took control. She recorded the names of the dead including Margaret. There were eight wounded six seriously. She told Triage that she would re-staff and re-provision in the games room to clear the backlog.

The next casualties to come on board were seven in a lifeboat belonging to *Gunbar.* The orderly wrote 'P.O. Moore' and 'Cook Emms' and assumed their ship was '*Gunbar*'. Shumack challenged this and the patients confirmed that they were from *Karra Karra*, picked up by a *Gunbar* lifeboat.

The next two patients gave their details as 'James Masson, Able Bodied Seaman, Australian Merchant Navy, 61', and 'Patrick Vincent O'Connor, Fireman, Australian Merchant Navy, 27'. The orderly wrote 'J Mason AB' and 'P. O'Connell', but refrained from writing a ship name. Shumack quietly realised that this orderly had just created two new crew members on *Manunda*. It was time she assigned him to more suitable duties. The identity of these two sailors has hitherto been a mystery.

CHAPTER 15
FOURTH RAID ON HARBOUR

10:32am to 10:40am

After circling around, 24 Vals survived to re-enter the harbour down East Arm three minutes behind schedule. Six were carrying a full load of bombs held over for *Houston* and *Zealandia*. The search for Houston was a priority.

Two Vals attacked the coal barge *Kelat* off Mission Point. A direct hit holed her and she was left to sink slowly.

On *Admiral Halstead* Johnson's machine gun team, exposed to Zero fire as well as dive bombers, coordinated and varied the intensity of their fire to trick Vals into releasing early while forcing Zeros away. Evasive tactics were less successful than before but the bravery of the machine gunners saved her. She absorbed some strafing damage without catching fire. Three dive bombers attacked one after the other, each with its last bomb, each tricked into releasing early. Near misses sprung a plate in her hull and caused some deck damage. No fire! It was the Admiral's day for miracles. The aviation gasoline did not explode.

On the south side of the port *Benjamin Franklin* was superficially damaged without casualties.

Small ships dispersed and zigzagging with skill made difficult targets.

Kangaroo, Warnambool, Karangi and *Vigilant* avoiding further damage were ready for rescue and recovery operations. The spare Boom vessels joined in. Survivors were straggling along in the fire-tide and some were heading for the Boom-net.

After *Neptuna* exploded many rescuers were suffering bleeding ears, all shocked and most unwilling to expose themselves further to the dangers of the port. The boat hand on C22 could not continue but not so John Waldie. He was singed and deafened by the explosion but his mind was with the poor beggars in the water. He turned C22 out through the fire-tide, tirelessly dragging sailors aboard, racing to shore with a boat load and returning as quickly as possible down the fire tide to scoop up more. He wasn't going to stop until he saved them all. That day the lives of 150 sailors were on the cusp of defeat. For them, John Waldie turned defeat into victory.

A Zero started a strafing run on the life boat and work boat from *Mauna Loa* but ran out of ammunition just before the rake reached target. As if she had been waiting to see her crew safely away *Mauna Loa* at that moment sank quickly, her cargo of military equipment with her.

Port Mar was beaching with difficulty against the turning tide and was starting to sink rapidly. Her life boats were shredded and the crew was facing a swim where sharks and crocodiles would not forgive wound blood in their habitat and box jellyfish were in season. It was then that *Gunbar* arrived and lowered a lifeboat to transfer the survivors of *Port Mar* to *Gunbar* and their wounded to *Manunda*. *Gunbar* took *Port Mar* in tow and helped her to beach.

A Val attacked *Katoomba* in floating dry dock but became distracted by shore fire. The bomb hit the water off the beach. Zeros and Vals were targeting the camouflaged fuel tanks with cannon and machine gun fire. The attack was too relentless for *Katoomba* to repel by herself. It was then that Lance Bombardier Frederick Wombey, 18, in charge of the Anti Aircraft light machine gun position, stood away from cover and opened fire relentlessly in the face of strafing Zeros and attacking dive bombers, adding sufficient fire power to drive the attackers off and save the oil tanks he was guarding.

CHAPTER 16
'ALL CLEAR'

The 'all clear' sounded at 10:40am. Lieutenant Oestreicher landed his Kitty Hawk despite a punctured tyre. When he saw the carnage on the airfield he taxied to a dispersal yard and left his Kittyhawk with three serviceable Hudsons. Rumours and fears of imminent invasion were creating a wave of refugees. Drunken provost marshals were reported later for looting shops; the town was internally raped and pillaged; military personnel were collecting their dead and wounded.

Zealandia exploded violently. She settled by the stern on the bottom of the port, her proud tall masts of luxury cruiser days still above water. The official report on The Esplanade Tourist Board said that *Zealandia* was struck by a large bomb which holed her and she sank immediately. This was impossible because all planes including Kates were long gone from the port. The better truth might be that fire moving across her decks reached ammunition left near hatch No.1. This detonated the cargo of anti tank shells which sounded like a bomb, holed her and she sank quickly.

Vals and Zeros returning to their carriers intercepted *Don Isidro* at 10:35am. Zeros and Vals strafed her. At 2:30pm nine carrier based dive bombers returned. *Don Isidro* had already rounded Mitchell Point to the west coast of Bathurst Island heading north. She was hit several times, bombs striking home in a sheet as she tried to beach. A direct hit set her on fire. Captain Cisneros put out a mayday call. Her engines stopped three miles short of the beach. With all life boats and life rafts strafed out of existence an hour earlier and the sea fairly calm Cisneros ordered all hands into the water to swim for it. Ten hours later survivors started to come ashore in the dark at Rinamatta Beach. As the night melted into morning, Cisernos made a count of heads: 84 had reached shore. Eleven were dead or missing, mostly the wounded who could not avoid some release of blood into the infested waters. During the morning the survivors watched their ship drifting ashore still burning until she foundered in shallow water.

It took the crew of *Florence D.* some time to pick up Tom Moorer and the crew of the Patwing 22 Catalina that ditched in the distance. They set course for Darwin and in the afternoon a mayday call summoned them to the plight of *Don Isidro*. The Japanese Vals bombing *Don Isidro* at 2:30pm spotted *Florence D.* at 3pm. As the planes were diving, Moorer on the bridge with Captain Carmelo Manzano noticed that Manzano was genuflecting and muttering. Moorer asked what was wrong and Manzano told him about the forward cargo of ammunition. Five misses and four direct hits later the bow of *Florence D.* exploded dramatically and she sank by the bow immediately. Three of the Filipino crew and wounded airman J.C. Schuler were killed. Captain Manzano was one of the seriously injured.

Moorer took command. He directed survivors into two lifeboats. Blown by the wind, they reached Bathurst Island around midnight. In the morning Brother Andrew Smith arrived in the mission lugger St Francis. He picked up Manzano, four who were badly burnt and six others whose injuries would soon be life threatening. With a full boat the Brother took them to Darwin.

CHAPTER 17
FOURTH RAID ON RAAF BASE

By Land Based Bettys and Kates
11:57am to 12:25pm

Group Captain Frederick Scherger made his way through the gate into RAAF Base. He started to organise a counter attack. At Darwin he still had three Hudson Bombers and at Batchelor 9 functional Wirraways. But the worst was yet to come.

At 9.58am, 54 land based long range medium bombers took off: 27 were Nells out of Ambon in Ceram and 27 were Bettys out of Kendari in the Celebes. They arrived over the Darwin RAAF Base at 11:57am for a high altitude attack each plane carrying one 800kg bomb and fully armed with cannon and machine gun. The aim was total annihilation of RAAF Base which took 25 minutes. *Platypus* sounded a warning as 27 aircraft approached from one direction at 18,000ft and another 27 from the opposite direction.

All buildings and facilities were demolished: all four blocks of quarters, all hangars and unserviceable aircraft in these, No. 13 squadron headquarters with all their stores and spares, No. 12 Squadron hangar holding spares for American Kitty Hawks, all hutments, houses and living quarters, all repair shops, fuel tankers, fire engines, ambulances, all Q-stores and their contents including parachutes, water storage, backup generators and finally, the large RAAF Hospital. Six Lockheed Hudson Bombers were destroyed and one damaged. Also damaged were 2 Kittyhawks, a B24 Liberator and a Wirraway. Six personnel were killed by this raid with many wounded, some fatally. This time the RAAF Base water tower was wrecked and the emergency power supply destroyed.

Some assets survived including Oestreicher's Kittyhawk and 3 Hudson Bombers parked remotely in a dispersal yard and, further south at Batchelor, 9 Wirraway fighters.

The situation for hospitals was grim. Berrimah and Myilly were damaged; RAAF was destroyed; Bagot, though strafed was operational; *Manunda* was damaged but still functioning. Evacuation drills practised with all medical personnel in the Darwin area were a vital asset in these circumstances.

On *Manunda* it was chaotic with eleven staff killed, 58 of her own injured, 18 seriously and boatloads of wounded arriving from other ships and the shore.

Clara Shumack had it under control, calling her nurses and orderlies together for revised assignment of duties, rounding up their own wounded, dealing with the arrivals from other boats and preparing accommodation for so many patients. She sent two orderlies to the store to draw fifty hammocks and start slinging these on the upper deck areas, the new ward for the walking wounded. She briefed chief radio operator Shacklock to bring messages to her promptly. When he reported the massive loss of hospital facilities on shore she may have told RAAF to use Bagot until she called them onto *Manunda* and disciplined *Myilly* and Berrimah to stick with the evacuation procedures as practised.

As Shumack passed through B ward she saw Masson and O'Connor whose names had been spelt incorrectly and their ship not recorded by an orderly. She may have asked which ships they were from. They both would have replied "*Zealandia*."

Manunda treated 58 of her own wounded, admitted 76 direct from the harbour onslaught, loaded the patients from the shore based hospitals and sailed from Darwin Harbour for Freemantle on Friday February 20th with 260 seriously wounded and 40 walking wounded. Her personnel included 15 trained nurses, 7 doctors and 100 orderlies.

HMAHS Manunda lifeboat on ferry duty - From the Collection of Petty Officer H.E.S. 'Nobby' Clark by courtesy of Major Faye Clark WRAAC (ret.) OAM RFD.

CHAPTER 18
FUSCHIDA'S PHANTOMS

Back on the Japanese flagship *Akagi*, Commander Mitsuo Fushida was thinking about the glorious victory at Pearl Harbour where his planes delivered a total bomb and torpedo count of 271. When Vice Admiral Osami Nagumo entered, Fushida bowed low. After the Admiral congratulated him on the day's success, Fushida spoke intently, offended that this target was not worthy of Nagumo Force. The only port installations were one wharf and a few waterfront buildings, the town was less than a village with no large buildings and undefended with Australian fighters spread over Europe, Africa and the Middle East.

Nagumo added that only 639 bombs had to be dropped. Fushida suddenly realized the magnitude of the day's battle. Nagumo paused for Fushida to do so. After a while, Nagumo asked Fushida if Sergeant Hajime Toyoshima was still missing. He was.

Today, Nagumo learnt that if the attack on Pearl Harbour 'awoke a sleeping giant' there was ample time to take Australia before the giant could dress.

As Nagumo pondered this thought, Ceram reported on their early morning's reconnaissance flight over Darwin. The plane's radio had broken down but what they were desperate to say was "No *Houston*".

Even before the attack on Darwin began, Japan's invasion forces at Makassar had already weighed anchor for Koepang and Bali. At midnight on Thursday February 19th Japan attacked Timor in strength landing troops and gaining effective control of the Island within three days. As part of the same action, Japan took control of Denpasar airport in Bali. No opposition was raised from Allied military assets remaining in Darwin that day. For many in Darwin Japan was 'staging to invade Australia'.

Two days after the Blitz Aubrey Abbott's administration was relocated in Alice Springs and Darwin came under martial law.

The damage to the main wharf precluded its use for fuelling and provisioning. Operating from the small jetties at the Boom-net Base below Fort Hill, HMAS *Coongoola*, a 34t motorboat, was busy as a lighter ferrying fuel and water to ships in the Harbour. She was using cool clean water on tap at the Boom-net Base, fresh from Manton Dam, delivered through the Navy pipeline courtesy of 'Chook' Fowler.

Fuel was initially rationed and many had claims to be first in the queue, including *Warnambool*. Moorer's may-day call had reached *Coonawarra* at 10:37am and *Coonawarra* raised a rescue call on *Warnambool* but she was too low on fuel.

Warnambool finally fuelled on Friday February 20th enabling her rescue mission to *Don Isidro* and *Florence D.* on Bathurst Island. While she was rescuing 73 seamen from *Don Isidro* a Jap float plane tried to bomb

Warnambool with 60kg bombs but missed. During the raid, Sick Berth Attendant D.E. Shelly, with no consideration for his own safety, continued attending the wounded while bombs blasted nearby and *Warnambool* was retaliating. For distinguished service in attending the wounded under fire, Shelly was awarded the British Empire Medal.

Port Mar, Tulagi and *Barossa* beached. The first batallion of the 148th Field Artillery Regiment, Idaho National Guard buried their dead, salvaged their assets and stood to. They were strategically deployed to Ballaarat in the Victorian gold fields.

William B. Preston had enough fuel to make it to Derby in the Kimberley region of Western Australia. She was attacked by a Japanese float plane but escaped undamaged. Lester Wood observed the spectacular colours of the King Leopold outcrops along the coast, ochre red and pink with streaks and patches of yellow and blue. He camouflaged his ship accordingly and stayed as close to the shore as prudent navigation would permit. The float plane returned for another attack but passed overhead and disappeared. *William B. Preston* arrived at her destination on Saturday February 21st, scraping her hull on a shoal near the mouth of King Sound. Waiting for her at Derby was Ethridge Grant in the surviving Patwing 22 Catalina.

Manunda sailed from Darwin at 11.30pm on Friday February 20th and arrived safely in Freemantle. Fuschida later said, "We did not want to hit the hospital ship and I was surprised when I heard what had happened. It was the fault of the Dive Bomber crews. I questioned them and they said they did not see the Red Cross, though I did."

After the bombers were gone, in the late afternoon, *Karangi* was sent to rest in East Arm. That night Harry Dale, who was still trying to complete his first letter to his mother, wrote, "Reckon they expected to find the USS *Houston*. I'm bloody glad she got away yesterday."

A stray bullet had struck the oil tank of Sergeant Hajime Toyoshima's Zero. The oil drained, the engine seized, Toyoshima glided to Melville Island and landed softly in the scrub. A single Tiwi Islander, probably an early recruit in the Northern Territory Volunteer Defence Corp, arrested Toyoshima, disarmed him, and marched him to the Australian Army depot on the island.

The army immediately organised two evacuation trains from Parap station, the second for 2:30pm. There was only one passenger carriage but freight cars and flat tops were coupled and loaded with passengers. Aubrey Abbott wanted exclusive use of the passenger carriage for his family and their belongings from Government House. That didn't happen. People evacuating down the road were advised to go to Adelaide River because, if Darwin were captured, the last turning triangle would be at Adelaide River.

Allied accounting of Japanese losses were 2 Vals to Oestreicher, 1 to Jack Mulholland, 1 Zero to Hudson, 1 to Grant and 1 due to lack of armour. Fuschida said he lost 7 aircraft with one pilot killed, 4 missing and 6 taken as prisoners. The Terone-Spedding kill at Ironstone might balance the books.

On Friday February 20th Arthur Drakeforde, Minister for Air in the Curtin Government, issued a press release, "A squadron of Japanese planes dropped bombs on Darwin yesterday. There were 15 killed, nine women and two men in Town, and 24 hurt." This was eventually revised to 243 dead, but unofficial estimates go as high as 1,100. The number injured may never be known but it was probably around 400, *Manunda* sailing with 300. Of the 30 Allied aircraft in Darwin, 23 were destroyed. Ten ships were sunk, eight in the harbour with 25 damaged.

David Ross was captured by the Japanese Army in Dili on February 20th.

The Officer Commanding 7th Military District (Northern Territory), Major General David Blake, his Acting Air Force Commander, Wing Cmdr Griffith and the Commander of RAAF Base, Squadron Leader Swan now had the logistical nightmare of 2,000 personnel and no on-site facilities other than trenches. Griffith was standing in for Group Captain Frederick Scherger who was still trying to mount a quixotic counter- attack on the Japanese Navy. There was no plan for these circumstances and these circumstances required an immediate plan. All orders were verbal. Griffith ordered Swan who ordered all personnel to "assemble at a point half a mile down the Batchelor (some say Daily Waters) Road and half a mile in the timber (some say inland) where arrangements would be made to feed them, and Griffith would come over and address them."

Ambiguity and word of mouth soon transformed the original order into *'evacuate south'*, the colloquial term for escape to Adelaide.

Thus servicemen swelled the field in the *Adelaide River Stakes,* when 576 personnel, 278 from RAAF Base, driven by highly exaggerated rumours of impending invasion, gathered their belongings, abandoned stations and joined civilians racing for the railway station at Adelaide River. Many got rides in cars or trucks and on horses or camels. One rode a bicycle and kept going to Cloncurry in Queensland. Another stood on the railway track forcing *Leaping Lena* to stop and accepted a ride in the engine room.

The other 13,000 service personnel held their posts: sailors with few ships, soldiers with one clip of five bullets waiting their turn to have the rifle, airmen without planes and nurses in bombed hospitals.

As civilians went bush, the ruins, once a town, were deserted, except for pilfering Provost, two chickens, a fox terrier called Snifter and a willy-willy whirling the dust.

CHAPTER 19
What Happened to *HOUSTON?*

Having broken the Allied supply lines at Darwin the previous Thursday and at Timor the previous Monday, the Japanese, on Thursday February 26th, had two invasion fleets, one at each end of the island of Java.

Admiral Karel Doorman was determined to destroy the main convoy and its support force, the heavy cruiser squadron under Rear-Admiral Takeo Takagi. In pursuit of this objective, Doorman immediately deposed his fleet to engage the Japanese at the eastern end of Java, and the Battle of the Java Sea began. Doorman had 5 cruisers, 10 destroyers, little air cover and unreliable communications; Takagi had 4 cruisers, 13 destroyers, ample air cover and reliable communications.

At 5pm the belligerents engaged off the north coast of Java, in the Java Sea. The Imperial Japanese navy won the first round, sinking destroyers HNMS *Kortenaer* by torpedo and HMS *Electra by gunfire.* Gunfire also left cruiser HMS *Exeter* heavily damaged. Destroyer HMS *Encounter* was detached to pick up survivors and Doorman withdrew south, dodging torpedo attacks and then hugging the coastline. HMS *Jupiter* hit mines and sank. The American destroyers including USS *John D. Edwards* had spent their torpedoes and were ordered back to Surabaya to refuel and rearm.

Doorman turned his four cruisers north and, without escort, made a final attempt to stop the invasion of Java. At 11pm the belligerents engaged a second time. At 11:30pm the Japanese sent a pattern of 12 torpedoes that sunk HNMS *Ruyter* and HNMS *Java* with both captains and Admiral Doorman going down with their ships. Doorman's last order to the two remaining cruisers was to retire to Tanjung Priok and then to Tjilatjap.

The two surviving Allied cruisers from the Battle of the Java Sea retired as far as the western end of Java, arriving on Saturday afternoon, February 28th. The Japanese amphibious landings were still in progress and the two cruisers boldly gate crashed at Banten Bay starting the Battle of Sunda Strait.

It was nearly over before it started. The Japanese destroyer IJN *Fubuki* was covering access to Banten Bay at the northern end of Sunda Strait and let go a spread of nine torpedoes. The cruisers just succeeded in evading these, and the torpedoes ran on as friendly fire sinking a Japanese minesweeper and destroyer, damaging two other Japanese destroyers.

The two Allied cruisers attacked, sinking a transport and forcing three other transports to beach while the two large Japanese cruisers *Mogami* and *Mikuma* stood nearby like large watchdogs.

A squadron of destroyers, the dog pack, blocked the Allied cruisers' retreat from Sunda Strait. The Allied cruisers fought side by side like cousins-in-arms against the odds.

At 11:36pm the Australian light cruiser, HMAS *Perth* came under gunfire and torpedo attack and sank at 0:32 am on Sunday, March 1st. The US heavy cruiser fought on alone scoring hits on the enemy vessels that now surrounded her. She damaged three destroyers, but took a torpedo and lost speed. Her guns kept blazing, sinking a minesweeper. Three torpedoes hit one after another, and gunfire killed her captain, Albert H. Rooks. She came to a stop. Destroyers then machine gunned her decks while she rolled over and sank, her ensign still flying. Captain Albert H. Rooks received a posthumous Congressional Medal of Honour. This cruiser already had two battle stars and was later awarded the Presidential Unit Citation. She was the 'The Ghost that Died in Sunda Strait'. She was USS *Houston*.

These awards were delayed because there were no witnesses to tell the story. Survivors from the Allied cruisers were sent to Japanese prisoner of war camps in Asia, and it was more than three years before survivors were repatriated. They not only told the story verbally, they brought with them paintings and poems.

After the Battle of Sunda Strait, the way was clear for Japan to take Colombo and end British Naval control of the Indian Ocean.

Some of the Awards for Valour

Postscript note: Clara Shumack was awarded the *Royal Red Cross* in recognition of her courageous conduct following the Japanese attack.

Postscript note: *Warrego* was awarded the Battle Honour Darwin 1942.

Postscript note: John Waldie, Coxswain, DCA, was awarded the British Empire Medal for his selfless courage rescuing over 150 from the burning Harbour at Darwin. These survivors included many of the 62 Chinese seamen saved that day.

Postscript note: Thomas Moorer went on to become the US Admiral of the Pacific Fleet and then Admiral of the Atlantic Fleet. He served as Chief of Naval Operations and became Chairman of the Joint Chiefs of Staff. He was awarded 40 decorations including the Purple Heart, DFC, a Presidential Unit Citation and personal decorations from fourteen foreign countries.

Postscript Note: The first battalion of the 148th Field Artillery Regiment, Idaho National Guard was awarded 35 purple hearts at Darwin. The five who spared *Tulagi* were each awarded the Silver Star for Heroism.

Postscript Note: The President of the United States awarded a Distinguished Service Medal to each of *Admiral Halstead's* machine gun team who kept her and her dangerous cargo from harm at Darwin: Fred Archibald

Chief Steward, Dale Baird Second Mate, Allan Currie Third Mate, John Haffard Able Seaman, Edward Johnson Master and Albert Milbourne Chief Mate.

Postscript note: When the war ended in 1945, HMAS *Mavie* was retrospectively recognised with a Battle Honour Darwin 1942.

At a reunion Robert Oestreicher received a gratitude plaque from the grateful people of the Cox Peninsula.

Seaman C.D. Scott of HMAS *Koala* received a DSM for courage and devotion to duty.

Other awards are included in the text of the story.

Acknowledgements

In 2009 Cambridge University's Tamsin Palmer taught me short story writing as an art form. I pray the style pleases her.

My patient, generous but business-like critics kept showing me the way. In particular, Henry Bartlett CMG OBE who served with British Intelligence during WW2; Lieutenant Commander, Dr Anthony Holley RANR, currently serving in Afghanistan, Ross Dunlop my detail reader; and Professor Peter Little, Executive Dean of Business at QUT my advisor on communication. Any shortfall in the quality of the story is entirely mine.

Net and Trish, daughters of John Waldie, gave me insights into their father's heroism. Dr Albert Thomason and Psychologist Desley Miller sharpened my understanding of human behaviour during an air raid. Younger readers Jordan, Dave and Vernon provided new linkages. I have used a recollection of the day told by Corporal Edwin Campbell of the 2/14th to his wife Zita and daughter Mary.

Andy McDermott, Director of Publicious Pty Ltd has produced and published this book with professional and artistic skill. Major Faye Clark has gifted me use of the photograph collection of her father, 'Nobby' Clark.

I recognise the knowledge of earlier writers on the subject and hope they find my story a fair understanding of their facts and a contribution to the better truth we seek.

Bibliography

Lockwood, Douglas, Australia's Pearl Harbour, Darwin 1942, Penguin Australia Classics, 1966.

Hall, Timothy, Darwin 1942: Australia's Darkest Hour, Methuen, 1980.

Ruwoldt, Rex, Darwin's Battle for Australia, Darwin Defenders 1942-45, 2009.

Grose Peter, An Awkward Truth, The Bombing of Darwin, February 1942, Allen & Unwin, 2009.

Google and Wikipedia facts sheets.

Various Australian Government Documents including broadsheets from the War Memorial and the Lowe Report, 1942, parliamentary papers 1945.

Various US Government Documents and US Navy broadsheets.

About The Author

John Thompson-Gray was born in Melbourne on August 17, 1942, son of a RAAF Pilot and a rag-trade Supervisor. He has two sons.

John went to Sandgate Primary School and Banyo High School in Brisbane where he matriculated, going on to degrees in Science from UQ, Education from Monash University and a Master of Engineering from Royal Melbourne Institute of Technology.

He was a cadet with the Bureau of Meteorology, Master at Scotch College Melbourne, Lecturer in Mathematics at Swinburne University, and for the next 25 years had a successful career with BHP Billiton.

Retiring early, he studied the Theory of Evolution under Emma Townshend at Christ Church College, Oxford followed by study at the University of Cambridge achieving honours in Macroeconomics, Public Policy and Literature specialising in the Short Story as an art form.

John is a member of Darwin's Defenders 1942-45 Inc. and has spent two years working on a story of the first attack on

Darwin. He expects the story will appeal to young readers inspiring some to read further and all to feel the significance Darwin Day has for Australia.

John's writing studio is in Compton Gardens, Aspley and he has a list of stories to work through.